PRAISE FOR

A HIGHER Calling:

SERVING GOD, HIS LEADERS, AND HIS PEOPLE WITH EXCELLENCE

*"***Elder George Fishburne Jr.*** and his record of premier service in the adjutancy has well equipped him to author a work such as 'A Higher Calling: Serving God, His Leader's, and His People With Excellence'. His innumerable years of faithful and diligent attention to the lost call of service, will forever be the standard and example servants to come will follow."*

Pastor Antoinne J. Wright
Senior Pastor
Shiloh Family Worship Center
West Palm Beach, FL

"This premiere project by **Elder George Fishburne, Jr.** *is long overdue. At no point in the continuing acts of God has the Body of Christ needed a reminder that servant-hood is critical more than it needs one now. For over 20 years, Elder Fishburne has dedicated his life and ministry to serving those whom God has ordained to labor in the gospel ministry vineyard. This writing will inspire, encourage, and direct those with willing hearts to meet the challenge of bearing the armor so that God's leaders might focus on ministering to God's people."*

Reverend Benjamin Carroll Jr., M. Div.,
Senior Pastor
Greater Antioch Baptist Church
West Palm Beach, Florida

"A man who has something to say is a man who was willing to listen! My experience has taught me this valuable lesson! **Elder George Fishburne, Jr.** *certainly fits into the category of a man with a 'Higher Calling'. His faithful service to God and others has given him priceless insight that will strengthen the life and ministry of anyone who reads this book."*

Reverend Andre Landers
Senior Pastor,
New Birth South Metropolitan Church
Atlanta, Georgia

*"***Elder George Fishburne, Jr.*** *is an able and committed servant whose instruction can only be a blessing to the body of Christ and those who serve within it."*

Dr. H. Beecher Hicks
Senior Servant
Metropolitan Baptist Church
Washington, DC

*"***Elder George Fishburne, Jr.*** *is a ministry gift to the Body of Christ. He truly embodies what it means to have a servant's heart and the significance of establishing covenant relationships. The professionalism he brings to the ministry and the spirit of humility that he displays to the servant's call is the perfect example of servant leadership. When it comes to servant leadership development, Elder Fishburne deserves five-stars."*

Pastor William Holmes Robinson
Senior Pastor/Teacher
Second Mount Vernon Baptist Church
Atlanta, Georgia

MINISTER SHERYL ANN CHILDRESS,

I APPLAUD YOU FOR YOUR COMMITMENT TO GOD'S CALL ON YOUR LIFE AND MINISTRY!

CONTINUE TO SERVE GOD WITH EXCELLENCE!

GEORGE F. SEBURN II.

5/23/2016

A HIGHER Calling:

Serving God, His Leaders, and His People With Excellence

ELDER GEORGE FISHBURNE JR.

TRIBUTE PUBLISHING
ATLANTA

A Higher Calling: Serving God, His Leaders, and His People With Excellence
© Copyright by George Fishburne Jr.

Graphic Design by Delaney-Designs
Final Cover Design by Delaney-Designs
Photographs by Olin Mills Studios
Book Layout by Delaney-Designs

Library of Congress Cataloging-in-Publication Data available from the Library of Congress.

A Higher Calling: Serving God, His Leaders, and His People With Excellence edited by Nathaniel Holmes Jr., Tremelle Howard-Fishburne, Ellyn Jo Waller, and George Fishburne Jr.

ISBN-13: 978-0-9792511-0-8   (hardcover)
ISBN-10: 0-9792511-0-9

ISBN-13: 978-0-9792511-1-5   (paperback)
ISBN-10: 0-9792511-1-7

ISBN-13: 978-0-9792511-2-2   (guide and workbook)
ISBN-10: 0-9792511-2-5

Printed in the United States of America

*I salute and honor my father, the late **George Fishburne Sr.** for instilling in me the character traits of hard work, commitment, focus, and perseverance.*

To the hundreds of men and women of God whom I have had the memorable experience of serving over the years, thank you for allowing me to minister to you through this humble call of service God placed in my heart and on my life.

And finally

To you who have the call of service on your lives....

Continue to do as Paul implores in

Second Timothy 4:5

"But watch thou in all things, endure afflictions, do the work of an evangelist, make full proof of your ministry."

Then stand back and watch God get every gift of service out of you, all for His glory and for your growth!

CONTENTS

Foreword by Bishop Victor T. Curry

Acknowledgements

Prologue

FOREWORD

The Word of God through Ephesians 4, verse 11 reveals, *"It is He who gave some to be apostles, some to be prophets, some to be evangelists, and some to be pastors and teachers."* What an amazing appointment – being assigned and selected by God to teach and serve His people, until His return. In the same chapter of this passage it reads, *"as a prisoner for the Lord, then, I urge you to live a life worthy of the calling you have received. Be completely humble and gentle; be patient, bearing with one another in love. Make every effort to keep the unity of the Spirit through the bond of peace."*

These verses are instructions as to how we should live and honor each other in the Kingdom of God. They are also a poignant description of what an effective armor bearer and servant must be. I am convinced that one of the most pivotal callings in the development of ministry is service to the Senior Pastor/Teacher.

An armor bearer or adjutant serves a key role in assuring that the man or woman of God's necessities are attended to efficiently, so that the work of God is not thwarted. No one exemplifies this more than **Elder George Fishburne Jr.** His leadership, keen ability to ascertain and meet pastoral needs, his social service acumen, and community concern combine to forge the epitome of service.

Elder Fishburne exercised his calling as an armor bearer for more than 20 years in service as my Senior Adjutant and Personal Assistant. Yet, his desire to serve God's under shepherd did not end there. He clearly exemplifies Jesus' teaching, which reflects, *"he who is greatest among you must first serve"*; as well as the teaching of the **Rev. Dr. Martin Luther King Jr.** who said, *"all can be great because all can serve."*

Elder Fishburne has tirelessly served visiting pastors, dignitaries, and persons of note from various walks of life in his aforementioned role at the New Birth Baptist Church Cathedral of Faith International. He has served prominent leaders including **Bishop Eddie L. Long, Bishop T.D. Jakes, Winnie Mandela, Rev. Jesse L. Jackson, the late Dr. Edward Victor Hill, Dr. H. Beecher Hicks, Pastor Jacqueline McCullough, Dr. Jawanza Kunjufu, Reverend Clay Evans,** and an array of others, constantly increasing my confidence in his competence, abilities, diligence, and faithfulness.

With the utmost respect, I have admired **Elder Fishburne's** professional spirit in the face of various personalities and last minute crisis'. No one is better positioned to pen a book like; **A HIGHER CALLING: SERVING GOD, HIS LEADERS, AND HIS PEOPLE WITH EXCELLENCE**.

The words herein speak not only to ministers or to those who are in ministry; but to the every day congregant. Surely service, when done in order, is Biblically mandated and essential to church and Kingdom building. Through personal and professional trials, **Elder Fishburne** has remained true to his Godly commission. It is noteworthy that he wears the suit of divine service comfortably and with great humility. He has learned to take the world's lemons and make the Lord's lemonade.

Moreover, he has chosen to live a life worthy of the calling he received from God and has done so in humility, gentleness, and patience. Truly, the essence of servitude and commitment can be found within these pages. I encourage you to read on and be edified by a lifetime of service, personal experiences, and faithfulness, personified.

Bishop Victor T. Curry, D. Min., D. Div.
Senior Pastor/Teacher
New Birth Baptist Church
Cathedral of Faith International
North Miami, FL

ACKNOWLEDGEMENTS

I take this opportunity to thank the many people who made this great effort a manageable, manifested, and a memorable work.

I extend gratitude to my God-Fearing, beautiful, and doubly talented wife, *Tremelle*. Baby, your love, support, prayer, and wise counsel have been a tremendous and unparalleled blessing. To my daughter, Mikayla, our 'gift from God'. You are loved, favored, and cherished. To my family in the person of my mother *Betty Joyce Fishburne*, sister, *Tammy,* and brother, *Chris* for loving me unconditionally long before God's favor found its way to my doorstep.

I extend heartfelt appreciation to several church families for your devotion to and discipline of me. In honor of the late Reverends' *J.J. Williams, J.D. Dukes, George Washington,* and *A.J. Mays,* all former pastors of the *Metropolitan African Methodist Episcopal Church* of Miami, Florida for teaching me to remember, respect, and revere a Holy God.

To the faithful people of the *New Birth Baptist Church Cathedral of Faith International* of North Miami, Florida and my spiritual father, *Bishop Victor T. Curry* for repeatedly speaking life into me. Sir, thanks for covering me, chastising me, and calling me *'son'.* To the *Elder George Fishburne Jr. Armor-bearer's Ministry* of the New Birth Church, your unrelenting and faithful service to God has not escaped His omnipresent eye.

To one of God's premiere and honorable pastors, teachers, musicians, and vocalists, *Reverend Dr. Alyn E. Waller, Mrs. Ellyn Jo Waller, Morgan, Eryka* and the saints of the *Enon Tabernacle Baptist Church* of Philadelphia, Pennsylvania, know that I am thankful for your unselfish wisdom, instruction, and timely covering. To my mentor in the servant's ministry, *Bishop Darryl S. Brister*, it is because of your living example of service that God revealed a *'Higher Calling'* tailor made just for me.

To *Pastor Craig L. and Chi'Ira Oliver Sr.*, as well as the gracious people of the Elizabeth Baptist Church of Atlanta, Georgia, your love and kind spirit is appreciated.

To *Pastor and Mrs. Joe Cephus Johnson and the Greater Ebenezer Baptist Church, I say thank you* for your words of wisdom and fatherly support throughout the years. To my *Godfather, Mr. Joe Cromartie, and Spiritual Grandfather, Bishop Eddie L. Long*, thanks for your continued prayers and guidance.

To *Dr. Mack King & Patricia Carter* of the *Mount Olive Baptist Church* of Fort Lauderdale, Florida for your boundless support and encouragement. Your tireless efforts of love and positive reinforcement saved my life.

To my *'village'*, extended family, and inner circle of friends: Elder William *'Gip'* & Lisa Gipson, Deacon Anthony & Cheryl Biggs, Deacon Kelvin *'Pete'* & Claudette Davis, Elder Byron & Adrienne Burnett, Elder Robert *'Bob'* & Dr. Anita Tyler, Elder Torrence & June Wimberly, Deacon John & Pastor C.J. Kelly, Terrance & Phyllis Randall, Karla Howard, Tremelle Hayman, Renee Alexander, Wendy Carr, Valerie I. Harrison, Elder Pam Smith, Emelda Wallace, Fred and Robin Glenn, Sabrina Adams, Barbara Forde, Elder Tito and Gemma Wilmot, Maria Moorehead, Jamelle Ross, Wanda Brown, Norman and Diane Jenkins, Attorney Richard Harris, Attorney Dana Tucker-Davis, Minister Michelle Washington, Deacon Kenneth Rolle, Thaddeus and Shirley Daniels', Kathy Dorceant, Fred & Rhonda Anderson, Dr. Mae D. Bryant, Eddie & Trina Jones, Alice Edney, Alonzo & Tracey Mourning, Udonis Haslem, Tamika Forde, Agnetta Delancy, Tanjia Alexander, Lisa Joseph, Jennifer Bell, Thomasina Wilson, the Late Dr. John A. McKinney & Rhonda C. McKinney, Elder Ingrid Bethune, Robin White, Elder Jeffrey Murray, Elder Veronica Bedford, Sonovia Slater, Pastor Antoine J. & Charlotte Wright, Barbara Gorham, Clotilda Holley, Yvonne Buckley,

Clotilda Holley, Yvonne Buckley, Frances Blocker, Clinton & Francine Williams, Pastor Benjamin Carroll & the Late Bernadette Carroll, Pastor Connail Johnson, Elder & Mrs. Willie Starks, Elder Joyce Henderson, Elder Anita *'Songbird'* Wilson, Minister Brenda Jackson, Lorraine Jones, Valerie Wooten, Georgette Adderley, Kimberly Greene, Nigel Lewis, Verna Gay, Jeanette Fields, Pam Shuler, Jackson Bowens, Ronnie Smith, E. Claudette Freeman, Kim Burrell, Dr. Marvin Sapp, Laurick & Kim Ingram, Lashonda Holmes, Dwan Vine, Leon & Barbara Ruff, Attorney Sampson & Helen Oliver and Tim Littlejohn. Thank you for your love, support, and encouragement.

To my *lil'* brother and longtime personal armor-bearer, Elder Nathaniel Holmes Jr., along with his wife, Talie, you have been such a tremendous source of strength and your faithfulness continues to both amaze and inspire me. Thanks to each of you for the *'light'* and *'Lord'* moments, we have shared, moments, which continue to keep me, centered in, and connected to the Christ.

To my 'plethora' of God-children; Kiyata, Chrissy, Marvelous, Anthony Jr., Anísa, Nicole, Briana A., Breana B., Kayla, Alíyah, Ryan, Danielle, Joshua, Edwelyn, William, Tyler, Carolyn, Grace, Gabriela, Giana, Nathaniel III, and Keith for inspiring me to laugh even when tears were ever present.

I thank God for equipping me to place in print what He had already placed in my heart!

PROLOGUE

Quite often, we find ourselves at crossroads that require us to make immediate if not life altering decisions. Decisions that will affect how we live, learn, laugh, and love. Depending on the level of importance of that issue, we may even become overwhelmed by the process used to reach that all-important conclusion.

When we buy a vehicle, the thought process associated with the intended purchase forces us to ponder whether it will be a sedan, sports utility vehicle, minivan, station wagon or even motorcycle. We must consider the color, body style, make, model, year, gas mileage, interior decor, sound system, and a host of other amenities. Do I want a sunroof? Do I need a luggage rack? Do I prefer high profile tires? Are window tints necessary? Is my taste for a stick shift or automatic? Are all of the above in line with my budget?

Am I looking for a new house? Do I want five bedrooms, four, or maybe even three? How many bathrooms will work me? Will a two-car garage be adequate? Should we select a rural community to hang our hat in or are we made for the bright lights and the hustle and bustle of the big city?

What type of tile and cabinetry do I like and can I afford? Do I need ceiling fans or central air conditioning or will we just open up a window and catch a breeze every now and then?

Even when we choose a mate and ultimate life partner, a certain focused prayer and vigilance should be put forth in hope of connecting with whom God has ordained us to spend the remainder of our natural lives. Will they be short or tall, dark complexioned or light skinned, will they have a head full of hair or will they be balding?

Women of God want to know: what are his interests, is he independent, what is his vision for himself and the family unit that awaits him on God's horizon? Is he saved or is he playing saved games? Is this man a giver or a taker? Is he a lover of God or is he a lover of himself? Will he respect my desire as well as the biblical precept so appropriately coined by *Apostle Louis Greenup, "No wed, no bed?"*

Men of God want to know: will she support me or abandon me, is she with me for my substance or my stuff, can I trust her with my heart? Does she want a family? What are her favorite foods, clothing, entertainment, and the like? Is she a worshipper or a watcher?

Think about it, we all make vital and significant decisions every single day!

So why is it that many Christians are confused about God's call on their lives with respect to ministry? Is the same aforementioned truthful and introspective soul searching for the things of the world done to seek clarification of God's call in and will for our lives? Are we committed to a focused and undeterred prayer life and is it a consistent part of our decision making process? If we can make a commitment to a deliberate method for selecting our earthly desires, surely we can do the same in search of our spiritual necessities.

Sadly, many of our churches rely solely on who my childhood pastor, the late *Reverend J.D. Dukes* referred to as the *"faithful few,"* in order to accomplish the vision-oriented mandate that God has set forth. In my ministry of service, I had the privilege of serving my pastor, *Bishop Victor T. Curry* for twenty plus years. My varied roles included but were not limited to confidant, intercessor, protocol officer, special project advisor, ministry leader, department director, sounding board, adjutant, armor-bearer *(we will discuss the distinction between adjutants and armor-bearers in Chapter 2)*, valet, driver, messenger, and much more.

Many might ask, what in the world was I thinking by accepting the weight of the aforementioned responsibilities? Frankly, I would often ask myself the same question. Amazingly, I have always been led back to the same conclusion.

The deliberation and veracity, with which I petitioned God many years ago to give me direction for my life and ministry, also had an unintended affect. God not only gave me direction, but He also provided me with strength, stamina, and focus to follow that very direction.

God's call on my life has always revolved around excellent service through the vehicle of pastoral care. My life and the accompanying call of God has always been aimed at service. I accepted a long time ago that it might not bring me great acclaim or a financial windfall but I would most certainly be in His perfect will.

Simply, God's mandate for my ministerial existence and possibly yours is crystal-clear if only we would listen intently to what He has to say. His voice speaks of **'A Higher Calling'** and we as servants of God are charged with the important responsibility of **'Serving God, His Leaders, and His People With Excellence'**.

1

AM I CALLED OR AM I CRAZY?

My life experiences in and around church began long before I even had any semblance of clarity about ministry or the significance of a *'calling'* on one's life. As best as I can describe it, I meandered about church, doing just enough to cause adults to leave me alone. I did what virtually every self-respecting Christian child was supposed to do in church in my day.

I ate candy and cookies during service *(often hiding the wrappers in unmentionable places)*. I passed notes of no real substance to my friends and more often, than not, cute little girls who caught my eye. I hoped and strangely enough, prayed that the dedicated and watchful eyes of the ladies on usher board number one didn't catch me, or it could result in corporal punishment...banishment to *'the row'*, sitting between God's doorkeepers and on indefinite lockdown.

During this seemingly insignificant period in my childhood, it would be on Saturday's and not only Sundays when I learned some extremely important lessons that redirected my life towards the horizon of service. My spiritually formulative years at the

Metropolitan African Methodist Episcopal Church of Miami, Florida provided example upon example of what it meant to be fully committed to a single-minded focus and set of ideals.

I recall vividly standing in the choir loft at Metropolitan, two Saturdays out of every month in *'choir-usher'* rehearsal. That's right, you heard me correctly. I attended two rehearsals simultaneously. Now, truth be told, choir rehearsal and usher practice *(no one ever seemed interested in pointing out the distinction between rehearsal and practice to me)* simply wore me out. Consider that from age five throughout most of my teen years, I was in church for three to four hours on Saturday's in sunny Miami, Florida.

While my friends were on the block riding their skateboards and bicycles, I was riding a pew trying to figure out the difference between an alto and a tenor. My buddies were playing street football *(the lamp posts represented the goal line although it seemed as if the poles were miles apart)* while I received delicate instruction on which hand to place behind my back while standing post as an usher.

What made this even more challenging in my young mind was the fact that we only served one Sunday a month. I must admit that the second Sunday of every month seemed to take three months to come around.

The significance of my perceived ecclesiastical prison sentence mattered not to me until one fateful second Sunday morning. As the junior choir prepared to sing, I noticed that there were some who were *'robing up'* to sing, despite not having rehearsed with the choir. My first instinct was to point out this injustice to someone in charge but when I thought further about it, it really didn't matter since we needed a few extra voices that morning. Lo and behold, when we started to sing *'I Must Tell Jesus'*, those who had ditched rehearsal for sun and fun, ***'did not know the words'!***

At that instance, I had the closest thing to an epiphany that a child could possibly have. On that second Sunday, in the middle of that hymn and with countless Saturdays in my life's rearview mirror,

I learned a very valuable lesson. You cannot effectively participate in comprehensive and effective ministry unless you adequately prepare and fine-tune the gifts already deposited in you. The many hours of rehearsal I invested were for the express purpose of equipping me for what amounted to mere minutes of ministry.

WHAT IS THE CALL?

We live in an age when people haphazardly toss around words and phrases without first understanding the totality of their meaning. Even worse, many fail to take those meanings and then place them into their proper context. When we talk about *'a call'* on someone's life, the Bible has quite a bit to say on the subject.

In Romans 11:29(NIV), Paul reminded those who were connected to the Church at Rome of the specificity of God's call. He wrote, *"For God's gifts and His call are irrevocable. He never withdraws them once they are given, and He does not change His mind about those to whom He gives His grace or to whom He sends His call."* The word *'call'* in this context is interpreted from Greek as *'an invitation'*.

I remember my wedding and subsequent reception, as if it were yesterday. God blessed me with my wife, Tremelle, a wonderful woman who is comfortable with me pastoring our home but at the same time is not afraid to address serious issues as they arise. As we put together our wedding guest list, we did so recognizing that financial restraints would not allow us to invite everyone we desired.

After making some tough decisions, we pared down the list to those whom we felt had made extraordinary impacts in our respective lives. The day went as expected until we noticed that there were people sitting at a few reception tables who were not invited! We chose not to make a big fuss but I can imagine that they probably were not comfortable at our celebration. I noticed that some people could not look at my new wife or me directly, because they were well aware of their transgression and trespass.

Their mannerisms were guarded, even as joyous music blared around them and those with invitations danced and celebrated. Additionally, our non-invitees could not enjoy the fabulous meal prepared for our guests because they were in fact not guests. They could not take in and appreciate the accompanying festivities, because they were out of place and not in our express will. Has God extended to you a divine invitation to serve Him in the ministerial ranks as a worker and witness, or did you invite yourself into a holy place where you will not be properly equipped, encouraged, or sustained?

SO WHO CALLED YOU?

I remember when I purchased my very first mobile phone in the early 1980's. It was a beige colored phone and it resembled a block of wood. It must have weighed at least a couple of pounds and its big ear and mouthpieces could be spotted from several blocks away.

Whenever you touched one of the keypads, they illuminated with lime green fluorescence. I was forced to carry it in my hand, because it could not fit in any of my pockets. I was so very proud of that phone and I took it everywhere I could. Even when I was not on an active call, I would put it to my ear and pretend to be conversing *(you used to do it to)* with someone on the other end.

Occasionally, I would check my phone to see if it still worked because there were periods when no calls came through. In those moments, I would use my home phone to call my mobile phone and then when my mobile phone rang, I would answer it.

There appears to be an epidemic in the Body of Christ's pre-ministerial ranks of those who say that God called them, when in fact they called themselves. My pastor would often remind us as young ministers *"if you just pick up the gospel ministry call on your own, people, problems, and pressures will make you put it back down."* Throughout scripture, we find evidence that before

God calls men to a work, He first calls them away from a work.

When Matthew *(also known as Levi)* was invited into Jesus' fold, he was taken away from his lucrative and disreputable enterprise as a tax collector. Luke was often referred to as *"the beloved physician"* to denote both his reputation and soon to be former occupation. Peter and Andrew were summoned from their prosperous fishing business in order to join the band of Christ. Essentially, you will know its God because He always seems to seek out those who are already busy doing something! He then creatively channels their energy, gifts, and commitment to a stream rolling towards His perfect will for their lives.

Those who call themselves run the very real risk of being left to fend for themselves in times of crisis and calamity.

GOD'S FIRST CALL

My pastor and father in ministry, *Bishop Victor T. Curry* is an interesting man. To hear him minister, you would probably think him to be gregarious and outgoing. I mean after all, he is influential in community and political matters and over the years has made his position clear on some very important and sometimes controversial issues.

The truth is though, as boldly as he teaches and preaches God's word, at heart, he is shy and unassuming. It was in 1984 when I told him that I believed God had called me into ministry, that he provided me with an interesting response. **He totally ignored me.** *I was crushed.*

After wrestling for months with what I believed was God's will for my life and sharing that jewel of information with him, he had nothing to say about it. To take it a step further he had the unmitigated gall to change the subject to sports or other current events. This went on for the better part of one year. Still, even in that time of what I later learned would be silent instruction, I held fast to what God told me and I would later find out, had also confirmed in Pastor Curry.

After he finally and publicly acknowledged my call, I asked him one day, why he had made me wait so long. He responded, *"Because God always calls us first to preparation."* During that waiting period, God was merely equipping me with the tools of patience and integrity, tools that must join forces with the call in order to fortify that call. Those who are called into ministry should cherish and make the most of those periods of preparation, allowing themselves to become thoroughly equipped by the Master. They are then doubly prepared to enter the ministry and mission field God has destined for them.

My high school social studies teacher, **Ms. Margaret Tate** always reminded us that *"Prior Preparation Always Precedes Performance."* This precept should remain at the forefront of our thinking even as we continue to walk with God.

Interestingly, during my preparatory period, God rarely seemed to speak to me. This was so, because He had already given me my instructions and now I was charged with the mandate of patiently waiting on His divine period to implement His pre-ordained call. ***Think about it for a moment.***

Have you ever had to wait on direction from God concerning a certain matter? It was then after serious deliberation, that you finally recognized that He had already given you the insights, talents, and fortitude to carry out the mission. Always remember that one of the most formidable obstacles to *'making full proof of your ministry'* is the enemy we call impatience.

JUST A 'WAIT' ON IT

Impatience often gets the better of us and we unwittingly abort the call all because we believe that God's celestial clock is running slow. ***Newsflash….God is never too early nor is He ever late!*** He knows exactly which play was called and when it should be run. Consider Abraham's plight as illustrated in Genesis 22*(AMP)*. In verse two of the aforementioned pericopy, God implores Father Abraham to *"take now your son, your only son Isaac, whom you love, and go to the region of Moriah; and offer him there as a burnt offering upon one of the mountains of which I will tell you."*

What is so striking about the text are two very important distinctions. The first thing God does is to tug on Abraham's heartstrings by gently reminding him that Isaac was his *"only son."* God's aim appears to be to decipher for whom is Abraham's love greater? Will it be for God or will it be for his son Isaac? Inherent in moving in sync with God concerning the call on our lives is the inevitability that we will have to make difficult and life altering decisions. Truth be told, some of us tremble when deciding whether to give McDonalds or Burger King our lunch money.

Can you imagine being compelled to choose between the God of creation and your own child? Now for once, don't go getting super spiritual on me.

What would you do?

For many of us, the decision making process would be heart wrenching. Yet in Abraham, we find a man who according to verse three, decided with apparent ease.

"So Abraham rose early in the morning, saddled his donkey, and took two of his young men with him and his son Isaac; and he split the wood for the burnt offering, and then began the trip to the place of which God had told him."

The second distinction almost blew me away, because it speaks directly to the essence of calling. The latter clause of verse two reads *"go to the region of Moriah; and offer him there as a burnt offering upon one of the mountains of which I will tell you."* If we fast-forward to the latter portion of verse three, we will find, *"and he split the wood for the burnt offering, and then began the trip to the place of which God had told him."*

What is most powerful about these words is, nowhere does it indicate that God audibly told Abraham where to take Isaac! We can only deduce that because *"he rose early in the morning"* according to verse three, that he spent time in communion with God in order to get what amounted to be only partial directions.

How often do we spend both quality and quantity time with God, not because we desire the niceties life has to offer? Our time of communion with God should be akin to breathing and our thought process must always be, *'Lord I want to be near you just because I need to be near you'*. The many insights and partial directions we get while in fellowship with Him are merely benefits of the relationship.

You can even find a parallel in your daily existence. My favorite breakfast restaurant in Miami, Florida was Royal Castle located in North Miami, Florida *(sadly, it was destroyed by fire in 2005)*. I had eaten there for many years and because of my longstanding relationship with the eatery, there were certain privileges that were afforded me every time I walked through the doors.

My hot tea was always poured without asking. The type of eggs, I would normally have had to verbally order had no relationship existed, were scrambled medium, just as I liked them and without one word from me. The wonderful staff there had essentially taken me in and because my fellowship with them was frequent, they came to a place where they knew everything they needed to know about my dining habits.

Occasionally, I would find an extra slice of bacon *(my wife is probably wincing right now because she knows it was pork and not turkey bacon)* on my plate, not because I earned it but rather because the relationship says it should be so.

Love relationships operate on a very similar and significant plane.............**Love is what love does**. Because I love *(agape-unconditional love)* my wife, every now and then I send her flowers, take her to dinner, and express in tangible ways how I feel about her. Love *(which is a verb)* can be found in action and cannot help but to always be doing something.

Authentic love is always in flux and cannot help but to be active and on the go. God's love for us is always in motion and is constantly doing something either for us, in us or through us. Each instance is appropriate in describing what transpired between God and Abraham.

God did *'something in him'* via giving him instruction and direction. This act confirmed for Abraham that it was in fact God who was in charge of his life and destiny. God also did *'something through him'* because now, Abraham's example of faith and trust would be passed from generation to generation. Abraham would forever represent the *'platinum card'* standard for faith and fellowship with God.

God also *'did something for him'* by salvaging both his son's life and Abraham's faith all at the same time. Because of his faith and communion actions, Abraham now occupies a prominent place in the **'Hall of Faith'** found in Hebrews 11: 17-18 (NLT): *"It was by faith that Abraham offered Isaac as a sacrifice when God was testing him. Abraham, who had received God's promises, was ready to sacrifice his only son, Isaac, though God had promised him, Isaac is the son through whom your descendants will be counted."*

Consistent and sincere communion with God always opens up to us the *'extras'* He has available to those who are in a committed relationship with Him and readily embrace the ministry mission agenda He has prepared for their lives. If you are trying to determine what call God has placed on your life, simply ask yourself this question: Am I in wholesome and meaningful relationship with Him?

GOD CANT USE YOU TILL YOU
COME ON DOWN

My pastor always told me that, *"the only way up with God… is down."* The high premium that God places on humility in carrying out kingdom assignments should not be lost on any of us. My thoughts often rush back to **Mother Rosa Allen**, who was church mother at my childhood church for well over 50 years. Whenever I was in earshot, I could hear her sing the tune *'Zechariah, come on down, Zechariah, come on down, Zechariah, come on down, God can't use you till you come on down."*

Mother Allen was really making reference to Zacchaeus[1], a chief tax collector and wealthy Jericho businessperson. Luke 19: 1-10 (NLT) tells us that while Jesus was *"passing through"* Jericho, He spotted the well to do Jericho resident perched in a tree.

Verses one through six read:

> *"Jesus entered Jericho and made His way through*
> *the town. There was a man there named Zacchaeus.*
> *He was one of the most influential Jews in the*
> *Roman tax-collecting business, and he had become*
> *very rich. He tried to get a look at Jesus, but he was*
> *too short to see over the crowds. Therefore, he ran*
> *ahead and climbed a sycamore tree beside the road,*
> *so he could watch from there. When Jesus came by,*
> *He looked up at Zacchaeus and called him by*
> *name. "Zacchaeus!" He said. "Quick, come down,*
> *for I must be a guest in your home today!"*

Zacchaeus quickly climbed down and took Jesus to

his house in great excitement and joy."

While Mother Allen's biblical reference was slightly off, the intent she attempted to convey was right on target. Whenever we think of ourselves too highly as it pertains to status, accomplishments and tangible wealth, God cannot use us effectively. Instead of paying homage to our God who bestows favor, we instead begin to think of ourselves too highly, thus minimizing God.

Note that it was only when Zacchaeus came down from his tree top perch of observation, did Jesus immediately put him to work. Even more encouraging, Jesus quickly came into his life and his home, which resulted in Zacchaeus issuing the following declaration: *"Master, I give away half my income to the poor—and if I'm caught cheating, I pay four times the damages." Jesus said, "Today is salvation day in this home! Here he is: Zacchaeus, son of Abraham, for the Son of Man came to find and restore the lost!"*

Note that in the background can be found the customary chorus of *'haters', (for the ebonically and hip-hop challenged, 'haters' refers to jealous people)* as Jesus made His way into the life and heart of Zacchaeus. Verse seven records: *"but the crowds were displeased. He has gone to be the guest of a notorious sinner, they grumbled."*

Always remember that while ***our critics matter, they don't count!*** They matter only in the sense that we should always be aware of and open to constructive criticism that will help correct our shortcomings. Critics do not count when our actions completely line up with God's Word!

The definition of humility as interpreted from the Greek language is *'one of low degree'* or to be a *'base thing'*. This concept is directly related to effective ministry in part because it removes you and me from the equation.

When you and I *(God's messengers)* become of less importance than the actual message, an ecclesiastical domino effect ensues. The recipients of our ministry now have an enhanced and unobstructed opportunity to become engaged by the effects of comprehensive and uninhibited ministry. They then become far less enamored with and distracted by the mouthpiece of the ministry.

John's Gospel account gives a stirring example of how God intended the act of humility to be free flowing and earnest. In chapter twelve, we happen upon the story of Lazarus who died in the preceding chapter. We also find his sister Mary, a woman of deep spiritual conviction *(Luke 10:38-39)*, who along with their sister Martha, the more practical of the pair, host Jesus the Christ in their meager home.

Scripture tells us that Martha served Jesus' supper, a meal she had prepared with her own hands while her sister Mary was otherwise engaged. You would think that Martha's care and concern for Jesus' appetite would win her Bethany's Nobel Peace Prize for Service.

Surely, her domestic and culinary skills would win her acclaim in Bethany and all of the heavens because she had more than adequately ministered to Jesus' tangible needs through her hospitality. Before we go heaping praise on Martha, there is an important element that should not be overlooked.

Verse three of chapter twelve reveals: *"then Mary took a twelve-ounce jar of expensive perfume made from essence of nard, and she anointed Jesus' feet with it and wiped His feet with her hair. And the house was filled with fragrance."*

Occasionally when my wife and I retire to bed, I will lay my head in her lap and she will gently stroke my hair until I doze off. Right at that moment, she does not run off and cook me a three-course meal, although that has its place.

She does not jet off to the nearest department store to purchase an expensive gift, although I certainly would not object if she did.

She simply strokes my hair. In short, often times, we complicate that which is intended to be so simple.

I have learned that many times, *'what we should do'* is often found in *'what we can do.'* God is not looking for an impressive ministry effort but instead He only requires that you and I work within our *'natural'* God given abilities and then He will add the *'super'* to it at the appropriate time.

We must discern in our lives what God requires of us at that time. Making the inappropriate move at the inappropriate time can be devastating. While we are in the act of serving, we must do so with focused and genuine humility. The act of humility we see exhibited by Mary in the aforementioned scripture is thus fortified and magnified because of both the simplicity and authenticity with which it was administered.

The scripture said that she *'took a twelve-ounce jar of expensive perfume made from essence of nard'*, which implies that it was accessible, and within her reach. She did not have to pause and go get it because she had already prepared to minister to Jesus long before His arrival. The act of sincere humility is often interrupted before it can be enacted because we do not sufficiently prepare to use this valuable ministry tool.

'Essence of Nard' makes specific reference to an herb often found in the foothills of the Himalayas. The part of the plant, which grows underground, possesses the rare precious oil mentioned in the scripture. Nard was warm and intense whenever it touched the skin and its soothing nature brought ease and comfort.

In biblical literature, nard became a general reference to all perfumes that were considered exquisite. In the Old Testament, it is referred to as a symbol of the intimate nature of a bride's incomparable love.

Scripture also tells us that the jar of perfume was extremely expensive for an unemployed maiden such as Mary. All told, the 12-ounce jar cost around $300.00 in contemporary US currency.

What she gave to Jesus cost something!

Mary seemed to understand the dynamic of humility personified and how it interfaces with giving on virtually every plain. Now, you are probably wondering, why was the perfume so costly? Interestingly, many scholars, including **James Rabchuck** believe that Mary was probably saving this perfume as it were for her wedding day, which made her sacrifice even more amazing.

When we give all that we have out of a sincere and abiding love for one another, it says that even though we could have cut corners, we chose not to. The essence of Christ is excellence administered through humility.

The cost and the content of this fragrance symbolized Mary's willingness to give Jesus Christ her very best but to do so in lowliness of spirit!

Scripture then tells us that Mary does something quite curious. She takes this rare and expensive perfume and proceeds to pour it on to Jesus' feet. This is significant considering the table at which Jesus sat to dine, was unlike the contemporary dining tables you and I are accustomed too.

In fact, the tables or *'anakeimai', (pronounced an-ak-í-mahee)* which means to *'lean or recline'*, were generally no taller than a foot from the ground.

As its name implies, those who gathered around it to eat, either had the option of leaning on their sides and propping themselves up by using an elbow or simply sitting on a cushion and leaning backwards, but this time, supporting themselves with both elbows.

Considering Jesus' posture, His feet would have been parallel to the ground, which means that in order for Mary to reach them, she too would have to lower herself. Even in a social setting like this one, Mary did not forget that Christ was not to be treated as a common person but instead she humbled herself by *'falling to His feet'* and then *'focusing on His feet.'* As she diligently anointed the Master's feet, nothing else mattered at that moment except pleasing Jesus.

Mary forgot that her brother Lazarus was also sitting at that table with the Savior and simply focused on Jesus. She did not seem overly concerned that Judas, the disciple of betrayal and the one who criticized her even as she ministered to Jesus, lingered near. Mary seemed oblivious to the fact that her sister, Martha who had just fed Him in the natural, now watched her minister in the spirit. Mary was lost and engulfed in serving Jesus!

How often have we ignored our critics and chosen to immerse ourselves in God's pre-designed work for us? It is only when we can tune critics out that we can then wholeheartedly turn Christ up. It is then that we can further pursue His tailor made call and perfect will for our lives.

Mary then elevates her focus to a new plain as she *'wiped His feet with her hair.'* This adds an entirely new dynamic to her efforts because according to Rabchuck, *"Mary was laying down her very self and her hopes and her dreams as a woman and giving it all to Jesus."* He continued, *"Mary's sacrifice of the perfume and of her hair was a deeply personal act of worship, done in a very public way."*

The actions of both Mary and Martha were admirable and were probably symbolic of the very first pastoral care ministry. Both appeared to understand the significance of blending humility in ministry and service *(although Mary's approach transcended the tangible).*

The latter portion of 2 Chronicles 34:27 (NIV) proclaims, *"because you humbled yourself before Me and tore your robes and wept in My presence, I have heard you, declares the LORD."* Mary, more than anyone understood what my pastor told me many years ago **"humiliation always precedes exaltation. The only way up with God is down!"** Anything short of full and complete humility and sacrifice is null and void. Jesus' supreme example of humility came in the form of his death, burial, and ressurection. *Will you humble yourself?*

ARE YOU STUPID OR SOMETHING?

One of my all-time favorite movies has to be Forrest Gump, starring actor, Tom Hanks. The movie is a satirical look at a young man who has been emotionally and mentally underdeveloped since birth but has been able to accomplish some amazing feats throughout the course of his life. Born with a physical defect that caused his legs to be mal-shaped, young Forrest can barely walk let alone run as an adolescent.

One day while being harassed by the town bullies, he breaks free and begins to run away from his tormentors, shedding his confining leg braces in the process. Throughout his life, he goes on to become a college football star, war hero, United States Army ping-pong champion and meets President's Kennedy, Johnson, and Nixon. Later, he tries his hand at being a husband, father, and ultimately a successful and wealthy businessperson.

The tone and tenor of the movie suggests that he somehow stumbles upon success and good fortune. Nothing could be further from the truth as he proves to be one who is dedicated, focused and not easily insulted *(because of his mental/emotional shortcomings)* or discouraged.

What is so striking about Forrest is his ability to simplify what others have complicated, a character trait that makes him so appealing. One recurring line, in the form of a question is posed to Forrest virtually everywhere he finds himself in life.

Whenever he approaches a difficult circumstance with compassion, love, tenacity, and focus, people ask him…..*Are you stupid or something?* He then politely responds with the same answer every single time by saying; *"Stupid is as stupid does."* He then adds, *"Momma says life is like a box a chocolates cause you never know what you are going to get."*

What I have discovered about calling and every Christian's

desperate pursuit of it is that it will cause people to ask you …
'Are you stupid or something?'

Essentially, they are asking you…have you lost your mind?
Those who are truly committed to the spiritual vocation created
by God for them will almost instantly find themselves lost in it.
True signs that you may already be walking in God's call for your
life could be some of the following:

- ❖ Do you lose track of time when engaged in your
  ministry efforts?

- ❖ Do you count the months, weeks, days and even
  hours until you will have another opportunity to
  perform it again?

- ❖ Do you constantly find yourself talking about your
  ministry endeavors to the point where you begin to
  annoy others?

- ❖ Are you so attached at the hip with your respective
  ministry that you are constantly recruiting others to
  join you in its ranks?

- ❖ From time to time, have you sacrificed your own
  resources to accomplish a ministry goal, even though
  you knew that you might not be reimbursed?

- ❖ When people see you, do they readily identify you
  with your ministry efforts or do they appear to be in
  the dark about what you do in the kingdom?

- ❖ Is your involvement so pronounced that even family
  and friends who are not members of your church
  know how active you are?

❖ Do you stay awake at night or become preoccupied thinking about how you can make your ministry more productive for and accessible to those whom it serves?

❖ Does your pastor or immediate ministry servant leader consistently seek out your insight and opinions for new projects and initiatives?

Someone once told me that you could almost assuredly identify the mission field God has designed for you. This is so because He builds within us an *'I won't be denied'* drive that both encourages and propels us when we get weary. The key is we must first tap into that ecclesiastical backing by making doubly sure that we are in God's perfect will for our personal and ministry lives.

For example, if I am not taking care of my family at home but I pay microscopic attention to the affairs of the church, then I am not in harmony with God's comprehensive will for my life. Although God still gets glory from my ministry work, I do not get any meaningful growth.

Do not be fooled, God has already equipped you and me to carry out the mandate. Life experiences coupled with time, will allow Him to develop us in the call and only He can and will work out the kinks.

You have lost your mind when God's focus becomes your focus. When we go deep sea diving into His unblemished design for our ministry lives, we then say to Him, *"Lord I trust and believe You will sustain me where You ordained me!"*

After over two decades of uninterrupted service to my pastor and the ministries God entrusted to him, I was able to say, yes, I lost my mind for the cause of Christ. In preparation for this book, I calculated the years of: travel, rental cars, itineraries, guest speakers, hotels, meetings, episodes of community unrest, strategy sessions, worship services, Bible studies, counseling sessions, house warming celebrations, hospital visits, crime scenes, weddings, receptions, wakes, funerals, hurricane recovery efforts, prayer breakfasts, luncheons, banquets, anniversaries, tent crusades, retreats, conferences, job fairs, conventions, symposiums, radio programs, television broadcasts, feeding efforts, clothing initiatives, rallies, marches, revivals, baptisms, baby christenings, special programs, sound-checks, concerts, hotel registrations, airport arrivals, airport departures and an assortment of other responsibilities, *(which we will discuss later),* and determined that I have been involved in well over **25,000 *(and counting)*** cumulative ministry events to the best of my recollection.

Success in your God designed and pre-ordained arena of ministry will ultimately be determined by your willingness to submit yourself to a life of focused discipline and humility.

The days of smorgasbord Christianity have long since ended and God now requires His disciples and servants to walk in the distinct trail He has already blazed and prepared for each of us. Running outside of our respective lanes poses many risks to the Christian.

When we get where God would have us to be, concerning our relationships, homes, families and houses of worship, He can then intercede for us as He did for Abraham and we too can avoid killing the rich promise that God has placed within both our view and grasp.

2

THE HEART OF A SERVANT

As a longtime substance abuse counselor and case manager, I have had the good fortune of assisting hundreds of men, women, and children, face and conquer the demons of drug and alcohol addiction. Their flirtation with and surrender to these mood altering and illicit substances has done nothing but wreak havoc in their lives, destroy their relationships, and leave an aura of uncertainty, death, and despair.

Despite the stranglehold that drugs, alcohol, and inappropriate behavior had on their being, many escape the snare and go on to live prosperous, productive, and meaningful lives.

Throughout my tenure, I have seen people grow through their dire circumstances and transform their lives and futures into blossoming gardens of success. What was once midnight has miraculously under the auspice of a mighty God, turned into mid-day. Amidst the many victories I have witnessed, there have also been stinging defeats and tragedies.

One such instance involved one of my former clients *(I will call him Samuel for anonymity's sake)*. Samuel, a 24-year-old young man suffered from a 7-year poly-substance abuse addiction. His love affair with the three *'C's'*, *cannabis, cocaine and Cognac* had a seemingly firm grip on his life and consciousness. He readily acknowledged his consistent and fervent consumption of the aforementioned substances but for the first time he also admitted his need for help.

Samuel's addiction was accented by several failed attempts at both residential and outpatient treatment. He had no visible support system and lived in transitional housing. Additionally, he suffered from a pronounced weight problem.

To compound matters, Samuel also suffered with a heart ailment. His condition often left him tired, despondent, and edgy. Multiple hospitalizations forced him to miss therapeutic group counseling sessions as well as individual interventions with me, his primary counselor.

Samuel had missed countless treatment appointments and the undesired but expected results were lost opportunities to work on sobriety and life skill goals/objectives in his established treatment plan. That treatment plan was created not only to identify relapse triggers but also to bolster his faith in God's ability to help him remain drug and alcohol free.

Throughout the cumulative two years spent with me as his primary counselor, Samuel made strides but in the end, the heart condition he so valiantly battled, won out. I often think about Samuel and I find myself doing inventory concerning my actions and wondered if I had done all I could to rescue him. After much reflection and second-guessing, I was able to reach one very important conclusion.

His heart failed him!

Quite frankly, if Samuel was ever going to remain firmly planted on the road of recovery and abstinence from drugs and alcohol as well as gain full and complete control of his life, it would all hinge on how far his *'heart'* would be prepared to carry him. Because his heart failed him, Samuel's ability to be productive in this specific life and death endeavor was limited and eventually proved fatal.

IF YOUR HEART ISN'T IN IT.....

Isn't it fascinating how we have a passion for and interest in some things while other things can barely get our attention? Have you ever wondered why you get excited about certain people, places, and even things while on the other hand an altogether different list of people, places, and things hardly even moves you? Why as a child did you opt for piano lessons over football? Why does the color purple catch your attention but green simply does nothing for you? You chose jazz over R&B, comedies over dramas, and the list goes on.

Embedded in each of us is a God-given passion for the one thing we long to do. Truth be told, we would eat, sleep, and drink this thing and it would consume a considerable portion of our thoughts, desires and time.

In most instances, this passion is unquenchable and often drives us to accomplish it by any means necessary. Always remember that God's design and divine call on our lives will most assuredly be related in some form to something that you have already been equipped to accomplish. That *'thing'*, will always be accompanied by an abiding passion and thirst to do it well.

Passion is merely defined as a *"powerful emotion or appetite"* and can be manifested in the form of either love or hate. Consider for a moment the thing you *'like'* doing. Could it be watching a movie or attending a professional sporting event? How about reading a good book or taking a casual stroll in the park?

Now, compare that to something you really 'love' doing.

Did your antenna go up? For one fleeting moment, you took the opportunity to reflect on your many life experiences. You thought about that *'love thing'* you are so good at and how it brings you immeasurable pleasure, satisfaction, and even confidence. You may not have recognized the smile that covered your face as you thought intently about the activity you are so very good at doing. The pleasure associated with it comes from a couple of places.

First, you take pleasure in knowing without the slightest fear of contradiction that you are not only good at something but rather you are *'great'* at it. In a sermon entitled *'Going from Good to Great'*, the **Reverend James I. Jackson** of Philadelphia, Pennsylvania points out that *"fear can never really be an option when seeking greatness in Christ."* Reverend Jackson's observation was on point in as much as the child of God can never allow fear and trepidation to become an impediment to pursuing our life's personal or ministry passions.

Because fear and faith can never operate in the same space, one will always win out over the other. What we believe to be God's truth in our respective lives will be the determining factor as to whether we will faithfully succeed in Christ or fail in fear.

Think about the confidence that Christ exhibited in every scenario in which He found Himself facing criticism or scrutiny. Throughout Jesus' three-year public ministry, He always stood firm and acted with complete confidence because He was just that, *confidence, personified!*

A shining example of that confidence is referenced in Matthew 12: 1-13 (NIV). From the outset, the Pharisees challenged Jesus concerning His disciples' [alleged violation of Sabbath law and protocol]. Verses 1 and 2 read, *"At that time, Jesus went through the grain-fields on the Sabbath. His disciples were hungry and began to pick some heads of grain and eat them. When the Pharisees saw this, they said to Him, Look! Your disciples are doing what is unlawful on the Sabbath."*

At that time, some Jewish teachers had corrupted many of the commandments by interpreting them more loosely than they were intended, but here, they had erred in the opposite fashion by interpreting the fourth commandment much too strictly.

The fourth commandment, found in Exodus 20: 8-11(NIV) reads: *"Remember the Sabbath day by keeping it holy. Six days you shall labor and do all your work, but the seventh day is a Sabbath to the LORD your God. On it you shall not do any work, neither you, nor your son or daughter, nor your manservant or maidservant, nor your animals, nor the alien (visitor or guest) within your gates. For in six days the LORD made the heavens and the earth, the sea, and all that are in them, but He rested on the seventh day. Therefore the LORD blessed the Sabbath day and made it holy."*

Faced with the law, surely Jesus would have to relent and admit that He and His disciples had acted inappropriately.

However, He did not.

Instead, Jesus tossed that very same law back in their pious faces by providing them with this reminder from Matthew 12:6-8(MSG). He retorted, *"There is far more at stake here than religion. If you had any idea what this Scripture meant— I prefer a flexible heart to an inflexible ritual—you wouldn't be nitpicking like this. The Son of Man is no slave to the Sabbath; He's in charge."*

Surely, you remember the schoolyard bullies who litter the landscape of all of our pasts. He was always the one terrorizing the smaller and defenseless children to no end. He would take their lunch money, push them around, and pretty much make their school lives unbearable.

I will pause here to say that in each of our lives, there will always be significant and defining moments in both our personal and spiritual lives. We must face the bullies, real and perceived, who continue to invade and operate in our God ordained space. When we face them, our confidence is bolstered and our Christ is blessed.

You might wonder how are we to face our critics who constantly hound us. I say to you child of God, that you have a Savior who will do all of the fighting for you.

The aforementioned confidence and courage we see in Christ is derived directly from His full and complete understanding of who He is. Because Jesus Christ is the *'only begotten son' (John 3:16)* of God the Father, His birthright of authority is automatically transferred to you and me as well as anyone else adopted into the family.

Knowing your position in and relationship with Christ serves as an agent of empowerment. Because you know that Christ specifically has your back, you could care less about what awaits you out front.

Think about the courage required to face those who stand in the way of virtually everything you attempt to do. They constantly mock and offer destructive criticism in an effort to demoralize and distract you. If they had the opportunity, they would not only attack your character but also your physical person. Still despite the odds and the ferocious attacks that stand in your way, confidence must be the order of the day.

The second pleasure found in your *'love thing'*, should emanate from a desire to be in the center of God's perfect will for your life. A good mechanic will tell you that when all of your spark plugs are firing properly, you will get maximum performance from your vehicle's engine.

In today's contemporary chariots, there are even computers affixed to the engine to determine when a particular spark plug or mechanical function is out of balance. Whenever we operate out of God's perfect will for our lives, essentially we are out of balance. Often it seems as if our spiritual focus is blurred and our mission unclear. We begin to wander aimlessly from task to task without realizing any substantive spiritual gain.

Sufficeth to say that Jesus' disciples witnessed how He responded to the hypocritical Pharisees and were able to gain strength from His unflinching courage. Not only will you benefit from the pleasure found in that God thing you have been called to perform but those who are a part of your life and enter your space at any given moment, will also become empowered to act in their own circumstance.

Additionally, when all of our spiritual spark plugs are firing properly, that too is a sign that we are in constant communion with God. This is significant because even as we operate in God's perfect will, our call will be challenged.

So is your heart in it?

I am not simply talking about whether you have made a decision to do the thing that consumes you. I am not even talking about whether or not this thing is anchored to God's perfect will for your life. What I am talking about, is have you made the effort to successfully merge the two?

What tangible efforts are you involved in that prove your allegiance to God's call on your life?

YOU CAN HAVE YOUR CAKE AND EAT IT TOO...

I remember as a little boy *(and even now as a man)*, how I would long for one of my mother's three layer chocolate cakes. I remember them being so delicious that I would tiptoe into the kitchen while everyone was asleep to help myself to a couple of slices, washed down by a Ritz soda *(I drank it warm because getting ice might wake up my parents and result in serious consequences and repercussions)*.

Whenever I would ask her to make me one, she would always lean forward pull her eyeglasses away from her face and say, "If you want a cake, I need you to go into the cabinet and get out the flour, sugar and frosting." I would eagerly obey her and lay out the requested ingredients on the kitchen counter.

I would go away and come back an hour later only to discover that those ingredients were in the same place in which I had left them. I would peek into my parents' bedroom, and there my mother was reclining in bed. If this were not so serious *(chocolate cake to a ten year old is quite serious and is on the same plane as world peace and saving the bald eagle)*, I might have laughed back then. Still, I went away, only to come back again and find that there was still no movement.

After several more trips to the kitchen and intermittent pit stops to my mother's bedroom, I finally dozed off only to be awakened by a familiar smell, the aroma of fresh chocolate frosting on a warm three-layer cake.

From those childhood experiences, I took away two very valuable lessons. First, I learned that quite often God desires to know how badly we want a particular thing before He commands it to happen. So much so, that He will place a portion of the burden and responsibility on you and me to bring it to fruition.

The second lesson I learned was that even when we do what God has requested of us, His ways are not our ways and His thoughts are unlike our thoughts. It was only when I left my mother alone to honor her word that the complete fulfillment of my desires were satisfied. In short, do your part, wait on God and then you can have your cake and eat it too.

DO YOU HAVE THE HEART OF A SERVANT?

One of the most poignant episodes in biblical writ provides a clear example of how the servants' ministry should look when fleshed out. The Book of II Kings picks up where its predecessor book, I Kings left off right in middle of the two-year reign of Ahab's son, the wicked King Ahaziah.

In 586 B.C., Jerusalem, the capital of Judah fell and was placed under the control of Governor Gedaliah by none other than the likes of Nebuchadnezzar. Jeremiah, believed to be the writer of both books reminds us that the dominant theme of II Kings centers on the principle that loyal, faithful, and obedient service to God will insure prosperity while disobedience will almost assuredly result in disaster and wrath.

The aforementioned backdrop is significant for it helps to give an accurate account of why both Elijah and Elisha acted as they did.

King Ahaziah had fallen from a ladder in his palace and as a result was stricken with an ensuing fever. He promptly sent messengers to inquire of the god of Ekron or 'Baal-zebub' interpreted as *'the lord of a fly.'* Single Baal gods solicited their powers from demons but Baal-zebub in particular was distinct in that he offered up a humming sound like that of a giant fly!

Elijah, at God's urging, promptly intercepted King Ahaziah's servants, and gave them a message. He told them that since the wicked king was so interested in seeking counsel concerning his life's fate from the wicked, that God instead had his answer.

The scripture reads in Second Kings 1:3-4 (MSG) *"God's angel spoke to Elijah the Tishbite: "Up on your feet! Go out and meet the messengers of the king of Samaria with this word, "Is it because there's no God in Israel that you're running off to consult Baal-Zebub god of Ekron? Here is a message from the GOD you have tried to bypass "you are not going to get out of that bed you're in— you're as good as dead already. Elijah delivered the message and was gone."*

King Ahaziah was upset and issued a warrant for Elijah's arrest. Instead of fleeing, Elijah boldly sits atop a hill, a feat amazing in itself considering he had once retreated to the confines of a cave for fear of being killed (I Kings 19:7-14).

This *'new'* Elijah would not be deterred by warrants, jail, or the threat of death. Elijah promptly called down fire from heaven twice to vanquish the men sent by the king.

The aforementioned verses give us a peek into the cracks and crevices of the Prophet Elijah's character. Despite this leader's many failings, he proved to be a man of honor and courage. Interestingly, it is not necessarily, what you see publicly in a leader but rather how he or she responds when faced with personal trials and issues. The once distraught Elijah was now standing tall in the face of God's enemies.

As we fast-forward to chapter two of II Kings, we find the very same bold prophet preparing to be taken up to heaven in a whirlwind by God. We do not know why God placed such a high honor on him because he too was a man and subject to failures and sin. Some scholars believe that Elijah's translation was merely a type and figure of Christ's ascension as well as the opening of the kingdom to all believers.

At that time, we are introduced to an interesting lad by the name of Elisha, who we know very little about. According to **Robert I. Bradshaw**, "Elisha appears to have come from a wealthy land owning family, if the number of oxen they had for plowing is anything to go by (I Kings 19:19). When the prophet Elijah arrived suddenly, Elisha's response to his call was immediate.

To demonstrate his determination to follow, Elisha dramatically severed his links to his past life by slaughtering the pair of oxen he was plowing with and cooked their meat over the wood of his plow. He then gave it to his friends and relatives symbolizing separation, change, and transition.

Scripture tells us that he then left and became Elijah's attendant or servant in a similar way, perhaps, to that in which Joshua had served Moses (Exodus 24:13 & 33:11)."

Bradshaw also implies that nothing more is heard of Elisha for at least the next four years, but we can assume that he faithfully and diligently served Elijah during that period and learned from him in the process.

"Knowing that the Lord was about to take him Elijah tested his servant's, devotion by asking him three times to remain while he went on in turn to Bethel (2 Kings 2:2), Jericho (2:4) and then over the Jordan (2:6).

Elisha and the other prophets of the Lord were well aware of what was about to happen and he refused to leave his master."

When they reached the far side of the Jordan, Elijah asked him what it was that he wanted and Elisha replied, "...*a double-portion of your spirit,*" indicating that he wished to succeed him in his prophetic office. Given the number of miracles that Elisha performed during his lifetime, it is possible that he was also asking for an even greater ministry than Elijah himself had enjoyed. Suddenly Elijah was taken away in a whirlwind and Elisha received what he had asked for.

What is so striking about Elisha was his immediate and complete surrender to his master's agenda. We find nowhere in tangible scripture where this servant or armor-bearer as it were, offered anything less than his unrelenting service, protection, and allegiance.

The heart of any professed servant is firmly anchored at the dock of unselfishness and is not concerned with when and where the journey will lead. They are only consumed with insuring that their leader has wise counsel and companionship on that very journey.

WHAT IS AN ARMOR-BEARER
WHAT IS AN ADJUTANT?

For the purpose of clarity, let us first draw the distinction between armor-bearers and adjutants.

Armour-bearers were aides chosen by kings and high-ranking military commanders for their bravery *(they were at least as brave as those they served)* and loyalty. As their name indicates, they did bear armor, but they were usually much more roughly equivalent to modern day personal assistants or *'aides-de-camp' (French for personal aide or camp assistant)*. One of the most well known armor-bearers of Bible history was young David who entered the service of Saul as the king's armor-bearer and was very good at playing a stringed instrument known as the lyre.

To illustrate that armor-bearers were at least as valiant and skillful as their commanders were, Saul's son, Jonathan and his armor-bearer alone successfully battled a much larger Philistine force:

"Do all that you have in mind," his armor-bearer said. *"Go ahead; I am with you heart and soul."* Jonathan said, *"Come, then; we will cross over toward the men and let them see us. If they say to us, 'Wait there until we come to you,' we will stay where we are and not go up to them. But if they say, 'Come up to us,' we will climb up, because that will be our sign that the LORD has given them into our hands."* -1st Samuel 14:7-10(NIV)

The term **Adjutant** *(a senior armor-bearer)* is taken from the Latin word **'adjutare'** meaning to aid or assist the commander. An adjutant is usually commissioned to lead a team of armor-bearers in the single-minded effort of caring for the leader and his family. The adjutancy was and is not a ministerial designation received through inheritance but rather by military or pastoral appointment. In contemporary religious circles, he or she also serves as **Chief Protocol Officer**, instructing in areas of pulpit conduct, apostolic order, and an array of other ministerial or leadership functions.

The single aim of the adjutancy or armor-bearer ministry is not to secure prestige or acclaim but instead to minister to and serve at the pleasure of the pastor or leader. They are charged with the responsibility of ensuring that an atmosphere of prayer, calm, confidence, civility, encouragement, and wise counsel always exist in the proximity of the Spiritual Commander.

NO HEART, NO LIFE...NO LEGACY!

Earlier in this chapter, we discussed Samuel, my former client who suffered from a heart malady that took his life long before he reached his prime. While it is true that the heart ailment that plagued him also deprived him of life, it also had one other unforeseen and subtle consequence.

It removed any possibility of a lasting legacy!

I believe that every thing God placed in us immediately becomes our responsibility to share and to get out of us. Over the breadth and width of our lives as servants, assistants, and confidants, we should seek to honor God by giving back to Him through service every gift and ability He so faithfully has entrusted to us.

Contrary to popular belief, it is not your thing and you cannot do with it what you please. Unfortunately, Samuel made the tragic decision to drink and drug his way out of God's ultimate will for his life. Because of Samuel's unwillingness to conform to God's will and transform into God's witness, his natural life was cut far too short.

I have heard it said that so much potential and promise can be found right in the cemetery. Every day, people make the false assumption that tomorrow will provide them with an opportunity to rectify the missteps of years gone by, only to find out that James chapter 4:14 (*MESS*) is so true as it relays, *"You don't know the first thing about tomorrow. You're nothing but a wisp of fog, catching a brief bit of sun before disappearing."*

So how can we be sure that our hearts are equipped for consistent service, while at the same time making full proof of our ministry? Throughout my tenure in the servant's ministry, I learned some very valuable insights that speak to this very important question.

God's perfect will for our ministerial lives is often manifested in part through how He functions in our daily lives. Sadly, it takes some people an entire lifetime to determine what that call is and how it should be applied in the tangible arena. The question of whether God has given you the heart of a servant can easily be answered by asking yourself an array of questions and responding in complete truthfulness and candor.

The ecclesiastical characteristics required for unselfish service cover a vast array of attitudal, commitment, and submission issues that only a God appointed adjutant or armor-bearer could adhere to.

DO YOU KNOW AND POSSESS YOUR LEADER'S HEART?

The heart of an armor-bearer should essentially be the heart of their leader. Interpreted from the Greek, the word heart is *'kardia'*, the root word for cardiac. The Latin correlative is simply *'heart.'* It means *'the thoughts or feelings of.'* The true servant is connected to their leader because they share in that leader's thoughts and feelings. When the leader is troubled, the armor-bearer too is troubled. When the leader is ill, the armor-bearer cannot help but to also feel the pains of discomfort and malady.

When the leader is victorious, the servant should also be connected to that victory and celebrate with the leader. The heart of an armor-bearer is not cluttered with personal ambition, goals, or agendas but rather they are completely committed to the vision of the house. They clearly recognize and understand more than one vision equals division. They also understand there is only one leader and that any other concept, structure or format to the contrary, is not God inspired, ordained, or permitted.

Ask yourself the following questions and see if the heart of armor-bearer, the heart of a true servant, lies in you.

Are You:

> ➤ Spiritually connected to not only your leader but also the vision of the house?

> ➤ Able to take directives from one of God's imperfect men or women despite the circumstances?

> ➤ A detail person? *(Did you notice the crooked necktie, the untied shoelaces, or the dirty eyeglasses, all of which may require your attention?)*

> ➤ A good listener and capable of deciphering your leader's mandates?

> ➤ Able to stand in a crowded room and at the same time remain invisible?

> ➤ A man or woman of confidence who refuses to repeat every thing you see or hear?

> ➤ Equipped to handle the chastisement that may come from your leader?

> ➤ Prepared for the criticism and jealousy from other brothers and sisters in the Body of Christ?

> ➤ An unselfish and consistent giver of your time, talent, and treasure?

> ➤ Of sound character and integrity that cannot be compromised?

> ➤ A fervent and consistent worshipper in private and in public?

> ➤ Constantly perfecting your gift through study and networking with others who also share this precious call?

> ➤ Personable and able to minister to the needs and concerns of God's people in the absence of your leader?

> ➤ Constantly seeking God's face concerning your ministry, family, finances, career, and leader?

> ➤ Regularly checking your ego at the door and acting in the spirit of humility?

> ➤ Well groomed and conscious of your appearance in public venues?

Often those unfamiliar with the call and mandate of the armor-bearer make the false assumption that they do nothing but *'carry the briefcase.'* While a substantial portion of their ministry encompasses physical responsibilities, God also charges them to cover their leaders spiritually. Essentially, God requires them to clear a spiritual path so that the man or woman of God may pass unscathed. Spiritual warfare for the armor-bearer is a frequent occurrence, because they serve as one of the last lines of defense and covering for God's leader.

The armor-bearer's willingness and preparedness for warfare in the spirit realm can be the difference between salvation and damnation for the lost. A true servant should continue to seek God's face as it relates to how they can more effectively intercede on behalf of their leader, his/her family, and ministry.

COMMUNICATION IS THE KEY!

The heart of a servant is one that fully understands the significance of discretion in communications. An armor-bearer's ability to keep the line of communication open with their leader is essential to cultivating a trusting and productive ministerial relationship. Quite frequently, the armor-bearer must communicate important and confidential information to and from the leader in succinct fashion.

The information in question will often concern personal matters relative to parishioners, errands, and family concerns. An armor-bearer should resign their commission if they cannot relay these messages with both discretion and expediency.

In most armor-bearer ministries, communication between the leader and the servant should occur within the confines of the established structure and not involve third parties.

The armor-bearer's ministry should be equipped with a senior armor-bearer, *(an adjutant appointed by the leader)* who provides guidance and controls traffic in and out of the leaders space. The adjutant or senior armor-bearer should always verify and re-verify any information before passing it on to the leader. Upon passing on any information, it should be legible, to the point, and occur with maximum discretion.

With respect to communication essentials, Armor-bearers should always:

➢ Remain polite and courteous with everyone.

➢ Interact with your leader within the confines of the ministry structure.

➢ Establish and maintain a healthy working relationship with your leader's Executive or Administrative Assistant.

➢ Be a man and woman of your word.

➢ Sow financially into your leader's life.

➢ Greet and speak to everyone you encounter.

➢ Smile…..it is not against the law.

➢ Identify and destroy the spirit of arrogance.

The armor-bearer who possesses the heart of a servant recognizes forthright that their loyalty and effective service to God, His leaders and His people is directly linked to whether effective ministry can and will occur.

Do you have the heart of a true servant? Only time will truly tell.

3

GREAT PEOPLE EQUAL
GREATER MINISTRY

I have always been an avid basketball fan and as a result, I often marvel at the success of the Los Angeles Lakers basketball organization. While the Laker machine has featured many awe-inspiring athletes and produced memorable sports moments, the *'Showtime'* squads of the 1980s were probably the most impactful. Consider the astounding numbers that these teams compiled during their heyday.

To date, the Lakers have won sixteen NBA Championships, five of which they earned in the 1980s *(1980, 1982, 1985, 1987 and 1988).* The organization can boast of fifteen Western Conference Championships dating back to 1972, eight of which were won in the 1980s *(1980, 1982, 1983, 1984, 1985, 1987, 1988, and 1989).* Continued examination of their accomplishments reveals, thirty Lakers Division Championships, nine of which occurred in the 1980s *(1980, 1982, 1983, 1984, 1985, 1986, 1987, 1988, and 1989).*

Even more telling is the fact that the organization has earned a playoff berth fifty-three out of the fifty-six years it's been in existence and never missed the postseason during the storied 1980s. Not surprisingly, they did not have anything close to a losing season during the 80s and during that period finished every year at least 25 games over the 500 mark.

From the 1979-80 through the 1989-90 seasons, head coaches Paul Westhead and Pat Riley *(Coach Riley would later win his fifth NBA title with the Miami Heat in the 2005-06 season)* guided the most effective of all the Lakers squads. Riley is almost assured of Hall of Fame induction upon his retirement from the active coaching ranks.

The cast of stellar athletes who have played for the organization and have been honored by having their jersey numbers retired include, Earvin 'Magic' Johnson (#32), Kareem Abdul Jabbar (#33) and James Worthy (#42), all of whom have already been enshrined in the Basketball Hall of Fame.

With all of its accomplishments, records, accolades and historical firsts, one common denominator links the successful 1980s Laker teams. That one common thread is the team of staff, athletes, and fans who rarely ever changed during that decade and contributed their piece to the puzzle of the Los Angeles Laker success and acclaim.

As I considered the complete concept of teamwork in the Laker organization, several themes continued to jump out at me. Those themes were **consistency, integrity, teamwork, foundation, and** *excellence*.

CONSISTENCY, CONSISTENCY, CONSISTENCY

Most business professionals will tell you that much if not all of their success can directly be traced back to the people they employ. Proper staffing has the ability to propel any entity to the apex of accomplishment or achievement but inadequate staffing can send that same entity crashing to the ground in failure.

I took the time to dissect the Los Angeles Laker team roster and discovered some interesting consistencies.

Hall of Famers Kareem Abdul Jabbar and Earvin 'Magic' Johnson played the entire decade of the 80s together as Laker teammates.

> Hall of Famer James Worthy played with both Kareem and Magic for eight of those ten years beginning with the 1982-83 season.

> The Lakers featured the same starting lineup of Kareem, Magic, Jamal Wilkes, Norm Nixon, and Michael Cooper for the initial three years of the decade.

> James Worthy replaced the departing Norm Nixon in the starting lineup in 1983 on a regular basis during the 1983-84 seasons and stayed there until his retirement in 1994.

> Michael Cooper, Jamal Wilkes, Mitch Kupchak, A.C. Green, Bob McAdoo, Mychal Thompson, Kurt Rambis, and Byron Scott were each with the team ranging from 3-7 years during the 80s and were viable contributing players throughout.

> Jerry Buss, a former real estate developer purchased the Los Angeles Lakers in 1979 for 67.5 million dollars and turned it into a 447 million dollar empire with annual revenue of 132 million dollars *(as of 2003 according to Forbes Magazine)*.

> Jerry West who served as consultant, general manager and executive vice-president for the Lakers, oversaw their ascension to greatness from 1979 through 2000. His likeness was silhouetted and is now the official NBA logo.

> Head Coach Pat Riley coached the team for 9 1/2 years during their decade of dominance.

Everything you just read screams consistency! The Lakers learned something *(and eventually forgot that something with the dismantling of Laker team featuring Shaquille O'Neal and Kobe Bryant)* that very few teams, businesses, and ministries ever learn.

Consistency is the lynch pin and launching pad for any long-term endeavor or enterprise!

Look at the contrast if you will. The Lakers dominance tapered off in the 1990s and resulted in four pedestrian seasons *(43-39 in 1991-92, 39-43 in 1992-93, 33-49 in 1993-94, and an improved 48-34 in 1994-95)*. In 1995-96 they put together a 53 win season which ended in a first round playoff loss but only after Magic Johnson came out of retirement to assist *(no pun intended)*. The years 1996-97 through 2003-04 offered promise as the Lakers won three Championships in five years.

After the 2003-04 season, **Shaquille O'Neal** was traded to the Miami Heat basketball team and the Lakers returned to mediocrity and rebuilding. As of 2006, they are still rebuilding and probably will be for quite a while because the legacy of greatness entrusted to them was interrupted.

The renewed chain of consistency created by these new generation of Lakers was now broken! The aforementioned chain of consistency and excellence created by the historic Lakers teams of yesteryear is nowhere to be found save **Kobe Bryant**.

When examining the Lakers success during the 1980s, one can see right away that they recognized that every thing they needed was already there. New pieces entered the equation occasionally but essentially, they learned to grow together and strengthen each other.

The body of Christ is overflowing with the gifts necessary to provide comprehensive, competent, and uninterrupted ministry. In our capacity as servants, we must remember that we have been equipped for this very ministry and must implement it with careful consistency. Our respective leaders should be confident that we will remain unwavering in both our service and our allegiance to the *'God plan'* for the house.

If everyone would play his or her role consistently, God would get the glory and we His children, would get the growth.

ARE YOU STILL HOLDING ON TO YOUR INTEGRITY?

Integrity is to the servant's ministry what oxygen is to each human being walking the face of the earth. Without it, your ministry will not survive. When we talk about integrity in the servant's ministry, what we are really alluding to is the servant's ability to adhere to a soundness of mind. A mind that is unimpaired and un-compromised.

A former co-worker once told me a story about her five-year-old daughter who exhibited this very soundness. She told the story of how she needed to go next door to a neighbor's home and instructed her young daughter, Jasmine, not answer the phone or go anywhere near the windows or doors. She was under strict orders to ignore any knock at the door and not open the door for anyone at all.

As the story goes, young Jasmine hears a knock at the door followed by a familiar voice telling her to the open the door. Jasmine responded to her grandmother *(who had given her keys to the repairperson who was scheduled to do some work on the house)*, "I can't open the door, my mommy told me not to open the door."

Grandmother patiently responded "Jazzy its Mom-Mom you can open the door sweetie." Jasmine responded again almost as if she were reading from a script "I can't open the door, my mommy told me not to open the door."

Visibly frustrated, grandmother makes her impassioned request once again "Jazzy its Mom-Mom baby, you can come open the door." Once again, the young child responded in-kind "I can't open the door, my mommy told me not to open the door." At that moment, Jasmine's mother returns and opens the door, letting both women in and quickly Jasmine's grandmother rushed to her side and asked "baby, why didn't you let me in?"

Young Jasmine responded in innocence "Because it was what I was supposed to do." We can learn a valuable lesson from Jasmine! The world, and more pointedly, ministry would be a wonderful endeavor if we would do what we are called to do and then stick by it with faithfulness.

One of God's greatest senior pastor/teachers, **Dr. Alyn E. Waller** who leads the wonderful people of the **Enon Tabernacle Baptist Church** of Philadelphia, Pennsylvania, inspired me with his message, entitled *'Keep Your Word'*, when he said, *"The gap between our words and our actions is called hypocrisy."* What Dr. Waller explained was that personal integrity should always usher the child of God to a place in our ministry where money, fleshly desires, and any other temptations cannot reach us. Without the strength of character and integrity alluded to in Proverbs 11:3, it is as if we have no moral compass and thus find ourselves adrift, uncertain of our mission, and unclear about the vision.

The aforementioned scripture translated by the Message Bible reads, *"The integrity of the honest keeps them on track; while the deviousness of crooks brings them to ruin."* It is when we allow external and nefarious forces to impact and corrupt what God ordained that utter chaos ensues.

An example of integrity maintained, would have to be that of Job. God permitted Satan to put Job's integrity to the test. Satan began taking away all of Job's prized livestock which included an abundance of camels and sheep.

Shortly thereafter, a messenger reported in Job 1: 18-19 (MSG) *"Your children were having a party at the home of the oldest brother when a tornado swept in off the desert and struck the house. It collapsed on the young people and they died. I'm the only one to get out alive and tell you what happened."*

Scripture reminds us that Job tore his clothes *(a sign of mourning),* shaved his head, and fell down upon the ground saying in verse 21, *" Naked I came from my mother's womb, naked I'll return to the womb of the earth. GOD gives, GOD takes. God's name be ever blessed."*

As Job endured these tragedies, his wife asked him probably one of the most profound questions ever posed to anyone in utter distress. In Job 2:9-10, we find this inquiry from his wife, *"Still holding on to your precious integrity, are you? Curse God and be done with it!"* He quickly responded, *"You're talking like an empty-headed fool. We take the good days from God—why not also the bad days?*

Not once through all this did Job sin. He said nothing against God!"

In his message titled *'I Still Believe God'*, **Pastor Craig L. Oliver Sr.,** leader of Atlanta, Georgia's Elizabeth Baptist Church, offered the following conclusion concerning life's trials and tribulations.

He said, *"God does not have to invite you and me into consultation concerning how he manages matters in our lives."* He added, *"Our confidence must be in God's purpose and his providential will."*

Personal integrity will not stop trials and tribulations from visiting your doorstep but it will embolden and encourage you throughout. The servant's saving grace concerning integrity is that we approach ministry using God's prepared design and subsequently we inherit His covering and mercy to escort us throughout the process.

CAN WE JUST GET ALONG?

One of the most underestimated and devastating enemies of effective ministry, is the lack of teamwork. This is so because it undermines the very fiber of Christianity, the fiber of fellowship. Those of us who continue in ministry believing that we are an island to ourselves are doing nothing but fooling ourselves and wasting valuable energy and effort.

Ecclesiastes 4:9-11(NLT) solidifies this observation with the following New Life Translation;

"Two are better than one, because they have good pay for their work, for if one of them falls, the other can help him up. However, it is hard for the one who falls when there is no one to lift him up. Moreover, if two lie down together, they keep warm. However, how can one be warm alone? One man is able to have power over him who is alone, but two can stand against him. It is not easy to break a rope made of three strings."

One of my many responsibilities at the New Birth Baptist Church Cathedral of Faith International was to host and care for all of the guests invited by my pastor, Bishop Curry. From the moment, we learned of their itinerary until they left in route to their next ministry destination, they were my responsibility.

I facilitated their transportation, hotel accommodations, and attended to their every need. Whether it was suggesting *(and transporting them to)* a favorite restaurant, a trip to the mall, attending to their offspring, and an array of other duties *(we discuss this more thoroughly in Chapter 6)*, I was their man.

As diligent and attentive to their needs as I attempted to be, it dawned on me during the spring of 1998 that I was merely one man and quite frankly, I was tired. I knew that if I continued to serve at the breakneck pace that I had been, I would burn out quickly and it would not be profitable for me, or the ministry. I also knew that because this segment of ministry was so intricately tied into me, that if something happened to me it could possibly hinder the important ministry of service performed.

Quite honestly, when our armor-bearer's ministry was formed, it was done so in part out of self-preservation and my desire to extend my ministerial existence. I had become so wrapped up in the aforementioned work that I was unwittingly being pulled away from God's original intent for my ministry life, which was to cover and serve my pastor for a season that ended up lasting approximately over two decades.

I noticed that when I welcomed aboard other men and women of God, who too had the call of service on their lives, the outcome was greater ministry. The teams' willingness to submit to my leadership had nothing to do with me but instead was a clear reflection of the group's connection to both the vision and the visionary of the house, our pastor, Bishop Curry.

Dr. Ron Gibson, Senior Pastor of the Life Church of Riverside, California exclaimed in his message, *'Balancing the Weight'*:

"Teamwork makes the dream work." Because everyone was on the same page, when it came time to turn the page, no one was left behind.

I began this chapter discussing the Los Angeles Lakers teams from the 1980s and how their consistency, teamwork, and structure contributed to their success and notoriety. Any experienced builder will tell you that no portion of a building is more important than its foundation.

FOUNDATION IS IMPORTANT

Luke 6:48-49 (MSG) highlights the significance of foundation in verses forty-eight and forty-nine;

"If you work the words into your life, you are like a smart carpenter who dug deep and laid the foundation of his house on bedrock. When the river burst its banks and crashed against the house, nothing could shake it; it was built to last. However, if you just use My words in Bible studies and do not work them into your life, you are like a dumb carpenter who built a house but skipped the foundation. When the swollen river came crashing in, it collapsed like a house of cards. It was a total loss."

Because the foundation of any entity is all encompassing, if it is flawed in any way, anything placed upon it will ultimately collapse. Know that the defective materials used to create it will waste away and thus that which is imperfect will not stand up to the scrutiny of time and circumstance.

Byproducts of the solid foundation found at the New Birth Baptist Church are the many wonderful, talented, and committed people with whom I had the fortune of working. One of the many gifted saints I served with was **Elder Ingrid Bethune**, my pastor's former Executive Administrator. Elder Bethune hails from the Bahamas, a very beautiful and vibrant island nation and paradise. She brought to work with her everyday, the outspokenness, professionalism, and creativity for which the Bahamian people are known.

One of the reasons Elder Bethune was so very significant in my ministry work is that both of us shared one important commonality. We both served at the pleasure of the Senior Pastor! We both recognized that at any moment, God could bring that season of service to an end *(as he ultimately did)* and so we sought to make sure that maximum ministry was accomplished while we could.

One of the very prominent errors that some Christians make is to assume that they have control over when the ministry mandate assigned to them will conclude. The Message Bible version of Philippians 1:5-6 says; *"I am so pleased that you have continued on in this with us, believing and proclaiming God's Message, from the day you heard it right up to the present. There has never been the slightest doubt in my mind that the God who started this great work in you would keep at it and bring it to a flourishing finish on the very day Christ Jesus appears."*

If you notice, God and He alone has full and complete command of whatever vision, call, and assignment He has placed in both you and me. We must simply decide to buckle up and prepare ourselves for the journey ahead.

Elder Bethune *(as well as **Tamika Forde**, my pastor's former Administrative Assistant)* and I interacted almost daily concerning an array of issues *(we will discuss many of these functions in Chapter 6)* related to the Senior Pastor's office and its productivity.

The New Birth Baptist Church Cathedral of Faith International is what I consider one of God's *'Flagship'* ministries. With that mandate, we were involved in an array of community service issues, conferences, and special programming in an effort to empower people and their families.

Elder Bethune spearheaded many of those efforts and along with the Chief of Staff, **Jeanette Fields**, provided my staff and I with itineraries and infrastructure to move forth in adequately hosting our guests. This is significant whenever teamwork is discussed because it is the foundation and structure of a thing that gives that organization, entity, ministry, business, and its people the wherewithal to successfully manage and accomplish its stated agenda.

Great people such as Elder Bethune and the plethora of others all over the world who are in fact the *'propellers' of ministry'*, are what caused lives to be altered for the better simply because, they remained loyal to the foundation from which they received their strength.

THE SPIRIT OF EXCELLENCE

One of God's most progressive leaders, profound preachers, and gifted vocalists is **Bishop Paul S. Morton**. Bishop Morton, the Founding and Presiding Bishop of The Full Gospel Baptist Church Fellowship offers spirit provoking messages and often ministers through song as a bonus. With so many gifts, it would lead one to believe that he got into line multiple times when they were given out.

He is friends with my pastor and has interacted with New Birth quite frequently. Whenever our paths cross, he often offers me words of encouragement and support. In 1992, I listened to an audio tape as he ministered from the subject; **'The Spirit of Excellence'.** His message focused on encouraging Christians to give our very best to God. In Genesis 4:1-5, the *'Spirit of Excellence'* is personified.

The Contemporary English Version reads; *'Adam and Eve had a son. Then Eve said, "I'll name him Cain because I got him with the help of the LORD. Later she had another son and named him Abel. Abel became a sheep farmer, but Cain farmed the land."*

The scripture continues, *"One day, Cain gave part of his harvest to the LORD, and Abel gave an offering to the LORD. He killed the first-born lamb from one of his sheep and gave the LORD the best parts of it. The LORD was pleased with Abel and his offering, but not with Cain and his offering. This made Cain so angry that he could not hide his feelings."*

Excellence insists that an unselfish sacrifice of our very best be a part of the equation. As we compare and contrast Cain and Abel's respective offerings, we see that *"Cain gave part of his harvest to the LORD while Abel killed the first-born lamb from one of his sheep and gave the LORD the best parts of it."*

The New King James version of Hebrews 11:4, further illustrates the distinction between the two offerings; *"By faith Abel offered to God a more excellent sacrifice than Cain, through which he obtained witness that he was righteous, God testifying of his gifts; and through it he being dead still speaks."*

The Spirit of Excellence insists that God will not accept as my mother would say, *"any old thing"* from His children! Producing excellent ministry service and other offerings to include those of time, talent, and treasure, is a constant reminder to God that we find Him ultra worthy beyond any man or woman.

The consequence of operating in prolonged mediocrity will almost certainly be the displeasure and disfavor of God. Excellence, fleshed out cannot be measured in terms of the splendor and enormity of our sanctuaries, homes, automobiles, bank accounts, clothing or even the accumulation of material possessions.

Excellence is actually a state of being. You can be excellent only if excellence has been deposited and nurtured in you. It can only be deposited and nurtured in you if you are in relationship with God!

Can you imagine how much more different our lives, families, and ministries would be if we'd placed a higher premium on excellence in service before now? How much further along in God's perfect will could we be? Remember, although Cain murdered his brother Abel, God's favor and blessing still accompanied Abel to the grave.

The 'B' clause of Genesis 4:4 (NLT) confirms this very point, *"The Lord showed favor to Abel and his gift. But He had no respect for Cain and his gift."*

I would rather face death with God's favor and blessing than to live aimlessly without His covering, guidance, and protection.

At the end of the day, will you be able say with confidence that you gave God your very best or will you know in your heart of hearts that your service was lacking and thus ineffective? The problem with operating in mediocrity is that after a while, you become comfortable there and eventually it becomes a part of your daily routine.

The bar of excellence should always be set high but often we set it to low and easily attainable heights. The lower the bar is, the lower the expectations will be. The lower the expectations are, the lower the outcome will be.

Because The Spirit of Excellence is really God's platinum standard for ministry, we must never substitute in its place, copper plated effort or service. Do not just bring your 'A' game, instead, bring your **'E'** *(for excellence)* game, and give back to God that which He has already entrusted unto you…***Excellence!***

Great and humble people cannot help but to do ministry along those same lines. The familiar Prego spaghetti sauce commercial hit the nail on the head when it coined the phrase, *"It's in there."* When you take an orange and squeeze it, the pulp, juice, and seeds have nowhere to go but out!

The very same principle should even apply when we face trials and tribulations. When squeezed by the pressures of life; ***consistency, integrity, teamwork, foundation, and excellence*** should be the ensuing response from the child of God. The time for ignoring your spiritual responsibilities has passed and now God is looking for a few great men and women who will serve with distinction, integrity, and excellence.

Your failure to use your gifts in the body of Christ is an affront to God and a drain on your brothers and sisters in Christ!

First Corinthians 12:27-31 (MSG) illustrates how great people are expected to manifest their gifts and reminds us of how important each gift is to the whole.

"You are Christ's body—that's who you are! You must never forget this. Only as you accept your part of that body does your "part" mean anything. You are familiar with some of the parts that God has formed in His church, which is His "body": apostles, prophets, teachers, miracle workers, healers, helpers, organizers or those who pray in tongues. Nevertheless, it is obvious by now, isn't it, that Christ's church is a complete Body and not a gigantic, uni-dimensional part? It's not all Apostles, not all Prophets, not all Miracle Workers, not all Healers, not all Prayers' in Tongues, and not all Interpreters of Tongues. Yet some of you keep competing for so-called important parts. But now I want to lay out a far better way for you."

Your potential for greatness lies directly in your willingness to involve yourself in Kingdom ministry. Whether it is in the servant's ministry, music department, evangelism team or youth ministries, your presence must be felt because the rest of the body is depending on you.

Always remember that *"If you always do what you've always done, you will always get what you've always gotten."* Subsequently,

"If you always get what you've always gotten, you will always be exactly where you are!"

We must make a concerted effort to locate and train the great and committed people lost in the mazes of our congregations. They must be infused with the battle cry for service, which simply says: **'Average People - Average Ministry, Good People – Good Ministry, Great People – Greater Ministry!'**

4

TRIPLETS

When I began my trek into the servants' ministry in 1985, one thing became readily apparent; *I had absolutely no idea what to do.* There were no self-help books or manuals that could guide me.

As far as I remember, there were no instructional materials concerning pulpit or ministerial etiquette and frankly, I had no clue how to jump-start my ministry. I knew that my desire was to be obedient to God's divine call on my life but I did not know where to start.

Interestingly, this is probably the plight that most of us have or will experience when faced with beginning our involvement in ministry, a new career, educational pursuits or even a new marriage. We know the mission, but are clueless when it comes to the method.

All I knew was that I was certain that God had called me for the express purpose of covering my pastor. It would ultimately become obvious to me that God had already prepared me and that the necessary learning resources were already on the way. The Message Bible's version of Ecclesiastes 1:9 made this painstakingly clear. It affirms:

"What was will be again, what happened will happen again. There's nothing new on this earth. Year after year it's the same old thing."

What this should mean to you and me is that someone, somewhere, has already attempted and possibly succeeded at what we are endeavoring to do. In laymen's terms, there is absolutely no need to reinvent the wheel. You should instead refine the wheel and make it relevant to the population you will serve.

As we discussed in Chapter 2, 1st Samuel chapter 14, clearly illustrates that unfettered service and allegiance to our leaders is certainly nothing new. In fact, men like Jonathan and Elisha perfected the craft!

Whatever ecclesiastical endeavor you have been called into by God, be assured that someone else has already done it and now your responsibility is to seek them out and earnestly take in their years of life experiences, monumental victories, and yes, even their colossal failures!

My pastor would always tell his associate ministers *"I want you to not only learn from my successes but also from my mistakes."*

Always know that authentic teaching and instruction is easily decipherable because it is hardly concerned with appearances or opinions. Genuine teaching and instruction goes straight down the middle of the page with no concern for personalities, egos, or private agendas. This was significant for me because my mentor in the servant's ministry adhered to this very principle.

Bishop Darryl S. Brister had the single-most important impact on my life as a Servant of God. Long before it became fashionable, he proved to be a living, lasting, and loyal example of what I have labeled, **'The Triplets of Service'**.

Whenever I think of triplets, what comes to my mind is the time consuming effort required to birth them into the world. These triplets, when properly nurtured and cared for should ultimately spring forth as viable and productive adults. The first Triplet of Service that I gleaned by watching Bishop Brister is the **'Triplet of Inspiration'**.

THE TRIPLET OF INSPIRATION

Amazingly, whenever I encountered Bishop Brister, *(at our first meeting, he was Elder Brister)* he always appeared to be in a state of perpetual joy. He always smiled and was cordial despite whatever venue he found himself. This perplexed me, because even I knew that not everything was always good. Surely, life had thrown him some trials, tragedies, and misfortunes yet his demeanor never betrayed those experiences.

So how is it that a man with so much responsibility, appears to be so unaffected by life's trials? How was he able to absorb the world's body blows and still serve effectively? What could it be that inspired him so that irrespective of his circumstances, he remained committed to serving his pastor, Bishop Paul S. Morton, and did so with excellence? The issue concerning his inspiration can be addressed with two responses.

First, let me be clear that there should always be an impetus for everything we do. The inspiration propelling our actions is quite often something that is heartfelt and has personally touched our lives.

The aforementioned triplet of inspiration will often take us past where our physical strength or ingenuity could ever carry us. As was Bishop Bristers', our first inspiration should always be our God!

Quite often, we mistake motivation for inspiration. The two are as different as night is to day. For motivation to occur, at least one significant and tangible factor must be in play. Motivation requires only that an external source illicit an internal response. Motivation says that you should get excited when the career promotion is offered to you. Keep in mind the offer of career advancement serves as the stimuli and your unbridled excitement is the expected response.

Using this train of thought, it should then follow that if no promotion is offered, then the exact opposite of excitement, disappointment, is sure to follow. Because motivation is based primarily on the aforementioned external stimuli, whenever the stimulus is absent, our joy and peace of mind will also be absent. Our responses to the innumerable challenges life will throw in our direction will be wrought with confusion and uncertainty, all because we lack motivation.

Amazingly, whenever an external or un-Godly stimuli kicks in, we become instantly motivated to act and perform that which a Holy God has already empowered us to do from the inside. Needless to say that whenever the stimuli changes, our motivations are negatively affected and God's work ceases to be done effectively.

Inspiration however, operates on a very different plane. **Inspiration** or 'thĕŏpnuĕsŏs' (*pronounced the-o´p- nyoo-stos*) literally means, '*to be divinely breathed in.*' For the Christian, our inspiration is derived from both an internal and higher authority, far beyond the reach of any external or carnal influence.

The aforementioned clarification concerning inspiration uses the very same definition attached to Second Timothy 3:16-17. The Message Bible's version of those verses proclaim; "*Every part of Scripture is God-breathed and useful one way or another—showing us truth, exposing our rebellion, correcting our mistakes, training us to live God's way. Through the Word we are put together and shaped up for the tasks God has for us.*"

When we accepted Christ as our personal Savior, the Spirit of God performed a dual function in us. First, He took up residence in you and I and then made it clear that He was there for the long haul and would never depart.

When my good friends, the Gipson family moved into their new home, I had the unique opportunity to see something amazing. As I entered the house, I noticed that all of their kitchen appliances were tucked into there corsets and the refrigerator full of groceries.

The bedrooms were set up and had been slept in. Clothes were in the closet and cars were in the driveway. The household was making the same statement that God speaks into our lives every single day. Simply put, we are and more importantly, God is here to stay!

The next function God undertakes is one that finds Him standing post in our lives. He stands erect and prepared to defend both our physical and spiritual person against any carnal or external scheme or device. Because *(as we have already learned)*, all inspiration comes from the Holy Spirit inside of us, that very source of inspiration must be guarded against any and all external ambushes and attacks.

The mature Christian should always seek to fortify and foster that source of our inspiration with a steady diet of Bible study, praise, worship, and fellowship with other believers. Whenever we encounter those who appear to be on a perpetual spiritual high, know that the high stems from an impenetrable connection to the spout of God-given inspiration!

The **'Triplet of God's Inspiration'** will not be denied!

The child of God must not allow him or herself to be lulled into a false understanding of where their inspiration is derived. That which is external should never be the sole and guiding factor in anything we do for God.

The Message Bible's version of Ephesians 3: 20 says it best,

*"God can do anything, you know—far more than you could ever imagine or guess or request in your wildest dreams! He does it not by pushing us around but by working **within us, His Spirit deeply and gently within us.**"*

THE TRIPLET OF PREPARATION

I have often been described as meticulous and at times quite anal to a fault, an assessment to which my wife and closest friends can attest. I suspect that these descriptions of me probably stem from the traumatic episode I experienced in February of 1985.

I was several hundred miles away from home attending Grambling State University as a student, when I learned that my father had died. I am sure we all know that whenever a loved one dies, a rush of emotions and even regret overtakes us. Such was the case with me.

My father, **George Fishburne Jr.** worked as a presser at a local dry cleaner and was one of the hardest working men I have ever known. Quite honestly, the only other activity he worked harder at was probably smoking. My dad put the chain in chain smoker as he puffed on cigarettes incessantly and often reminded me *"you've got to die from something one day."* He finally succumbed to emphysema and left me devastated.

His death caught me unprepared and I was uncertain of how to deal with it or what the aftermath would bring. I struggled intensely with his departure until April of 1985; when my pastor and *'spiritual father'*, **Bishop Victor T. Curry** acknowledged my call into the gospel ministry.

In chapter one, I expressed to you how God used my pastor to alter forever my view of and approach to comprehensive ministry. His message centered on how God has equipped each of us for service. Before we begin any ministry effort, we should always remember as was alluded to in chapter 1, *"God first calls us to preparation."*

The death of my father coupled with my pastor's insightful and timely words found me pledging to never again to be unprepared to meet any challenge directed my way.

Suddenly everything around me became a classroom and I found myself in a virtual and perpetual learning mode. I began to watch people closely to determine how and why they did whatever they did. I did this for the express purpose of learning what to do and not to do in whatever circumstance I found myself.

I watched as my pastor would study and prepare to minister on Tuesdays at Bible study and for Sunday worship services. I observed Bishop Brister as he cared for and served Bishop Morton and how he also meticulously facilitated the worship experience for the Full Gospel Baptist Church Fellowship events just as a skilled conductor would a symphony orchestra!

I have had the opportunity to serve many leaders in religion, commerce, politics, community service, education, and professional athletics, many of whom were regularly in my sphere of influence at an early ministry age. I learned from the many men and women I served, attributes related to planning, inductive/deductive logic and reasoning, infrastructure, goal planning and an array of other tools that shaped my thought process. I discovered that many churches and other entities have both human and fiscal resources but no comprehensive plan on how and when to use them for the maximum benefit to the people they serve.

I began to understand that the aforementioned tools of preparation would be the lifeblood for everything I hoped to accomplish in life.

How right I was!

As we foray into ministry or for that matter, any other endeavor, know that preparation is your insurance policy. Identifying the required resources needed for the task, establishing a protocol, determining primary, secondary, and tertiary fallback timetables, and determining proper staffing levels are essential to the success of your plan.

From an emotional perspective, preparation also has its benefits. When we have a clearly outlined plan of action, it automatically removes potential anxiety and frustration from the equation. The stress normally associated with implementing a plan is thereby diminished because the plan itself has been well thought out and contingencies have been built in to ensure success.

The precept of preparation is Biblical in its origin and has its foundation in scripture. The 14th Chapter of the Gospel of John (CEV) reads in verses one through three," *Jesus said to His disciples, "Don't be worried! Have faith in God and have faith in Me. There are many rooms in My Father's house. I wouldn't tell you this, unless it was true. I am going there to prepare a place for each of you. After I have done this, I will come back and take you with Me. Then we will be together."*

Interpreted from Greek, the word *'prepare'* literally refers to internal fitness and implies that construction and building are occurring. The act of preparation involves devising innovative and sound methods for pursuing not only ministry endeavors but also, educational, business, and any other pursuit, or interest.

My God-sister and one of my very best friends, **Adrienne Burnett** is probably one of the most talented persons I know. She has been in the field of education for as long as I can remember and for a time, she home schooled her children. She readily admits enjoying the work but once I had the opportunity to witness her true gift and passion.

While touring the new home, that she and her husband **Byron** had purchased, she freely told me about their plans for the kitchen, bedrooms, and the remainder of the house. Interestingly she had even made a preliminary determination about the color scheme, motif, and other technical aspects of what it would take to bring their dream to pass. Adrienne identified all of the required tools such as paint, brushes, and the like in order to accomplish the goals she and her husband had established. That was the last time we talked about it until I visited the Burnett home almost two months later.

The place looks like it was freshly cut from the pages of Better Homes and Gardens. The Burnett family decorating agenda moved from *inspiration* to *preparation* and finally to *activation*.......

THE TRIPLET OF ACTIVATION

As a child, I was an action movie lover and lived for episodes of a widely popular television series titled **The 'A' Team.** What was so interesting about this cast of misfit mercenaries was that they all came from diverse backgrounds, brought different talents to the table and yet were pretty much able to accomplish everything they set out to do. Consider the roster of the show's four main characters.

Murdock, the paranoid and sometimes delusional pilot, was quite strange. Yet when his *teammates* needed him, he would always swoop in and fly them away to safety.

Face, the smooth talking and suave con man, could get himself out of most conflicts because of his good looks and gift of conversation. His unique ability to use his attributes to get himself and his *teammates* out of the tight spots in which they found themselves was invaluable.

B.A. Baracus, the brawny and flight challenged tough guy, often used his physical strength to fight his way out of the many dilemmas that he and his *teammates* faced. His fearlessness *(except when it came to flying)* played an instrumental role in the team's success.

Finally, **Hannibal**, the *team's* cigar chomping and creative leader, often devised plan after plan shaped around their respective mission. While his methods and leadership could be described as unorthodox, his *team* trusted him unconditionally with their lives. Hannibal's signature response every time the *team* successfully completed its mission would always be *"I love it when a plan comes together!"*

Contrary to some misguided beliefs, **inspiration** and even **preparation** are not the endgame. The goal should now shift to causing the *'the plan to come together."* One of the more costly errors that we make as Christian laborers is to believe that once we have received inspiration and have adequately prepared for the task that we have accomplished our goal.

Nowhere in scripture or even in secular circles can I find where you get brownie points for completing a portion of your task. The joy and reward is in total completion of what God has placed in your hands and heart to do!

Even God abhors not seeing a task through and reminds us in scripture that He is not a quitter. The Message Bible version of Philippians 1:6 assures us of that fact with these words; *"There has never been the slightest doubt in my mind that the God who started this great work in you would keep at it and bring it to a flourishing finish on the very day Christ Jesus appears."*

The work God has breathed in you and me through *inspiration* and organized through us via the practice of *preparation*, has an intended goal and objective, which is *activation*!

No matter how you cut it, the work has to get done!

The due diligence you exhibited, or lack thereof during your period of preparation, will become obvious as you begin implementation. Whether you conducted a thorough assessment of the resources, people, and infrastructure you will need to accomplish the mandate will become either joyfully or painfully obvious very quickly.

There are a few insights that I would like to share with you concerning how to activate your ministry or business plan.

*SEE THE PLAN - First, make sure that you have a complete grasp of the plan yourself. Be prepared to recite and share the essence of each action element and goal. People need to be assured that you, the lead servant know and have complete confidence in the plan to be implemented. This is a good place to make sure that all components have been well thought out and any preliminary flaws identified and corrected. At least two contingency plans should be created in the event they are needed.

*SOW THE PLAN – A vital element attached to knowing the plan involves sharing that plan and how it should go forth with key members of the ministry who will aid you in carrying it out. Sow into them your confidence and trust. This should ultimately flesh itself out into a committed and focused work product. The old adage that you should *'keep your friends close and your enemy's closer'* has never worked in my experience. Those whom are not deemed trustworthy should not handle intimate and delicate details of the vision.

*SHARE THE PLAN – Next, the plan should be articulated to the faithful and dedicated persons who will carry out the mandate on the front line. Whenever possible, audio and visual aids should be used to convey the full scope and focus of the mission.

The Amplified Bible Version of Habakkuk 2:2-3 remind us; *"And the Lord answered me and said, Write the vision and engrave it so plainly upon tablets that everyone who passes may [be able to] read [it easily and quickly] as he hastens by. For the vision is yet for an appointed time and it hastens to the end [fulfillment]; it will not deceive or disappoint. Though it tarry, wait [earnestly] for it, because it will surely come; it will not be behindhand on its appointed day."*

During this phase, people should be encouraged to offer suggestions concerning style but not substance. The substance of the plan was introduced during inspiration and fine tuned during preparation. The substance of what God instructs us to do is non-negotiable but the style and method used to accomplish it is open for discussion.

*SEAL THE PLAN – Everyone must leave the room understanding that the plan has been sealed and is ready for its initial phase of activation. During this phase, assignments have been delegated and people are clear as to their responsibilities and protocol associated with them. Those deemed unfit to carry out their portion of the should be replaced at this juncture.

*START THE PLAN – Everyone should begin carrying out their respective responsibilities with a mechanism in place that allows them to report either incremental victories or temporary setbacks. Document these instances and make them part of the permanent plan record for future reference. It is also late in this phase that instances may arise when team and assignment leaders may have to be replaced due to unforeseen circumstances. Additionally, contingency plans may have to be implemented during this phase.

We should always adhere to the *'buddy system'* of ministry and appoint assistant/alternate team or assignment leaders. Selecting *'scribes'* to coherently record and preserve in writing everything that occurs is also advisable. This will ensure continuity of the ministry effort in the event leadership changes occur.

*SCORE & SAVE THE PLAN – Upon completion of the ministry effort, any notes, constructive criticisms, and comments should be heard, received, and evaluated. This is essential because it provides a tool to assess how well you fleshed out what God placed in you.

Additionally, it also creates a record for those who will come after you and gives them firsthand insight concerning your activities and a virtual how to guide to ministry. If you continue to be unsure after reading this chapter as to whether the

'Triplets of Effective Ministry' are in operation in your life, here are some honest questions to ask yourself:

Are You:

> Amenable to hearing what God has to say to you concerning not only your spiritual growth and development but also your finances, relationships, career goals, and other areas of your life?

- Comfortable with the team you have assembled *(are they trustworthy, competent, and clear about your expectations for them)*?

- A person of integrity who will see the plan through despite the possibility of temporary setbacks, failures, and unforeseen challenges?

- In God's perfect will with respect to your local church *(did God send you there or did you send yourself)*?

- Involved in specific and consistent periods of personal Bible study, prayer, meditation, and fellowship with other believers, for the purpose of hearing from God?

- Clear concerning the differences between motivation and God's inspiration and how those differences are explained in scripture?

- Comfortable doing what God instructs you to do even though family and close friends may not understand or even support your efforts?

- Committed to the vision of the house and in harmony with that vision?

- Committed to thoroughly examine the nuances of your plan and have you prepared a contingency in the event one is needed?

> An organizer and if not, have you added to your team, people who are and have other gifts which they are prepared to use for purposes of ministry?

> In possession of a method to evaluate the ongoing progress of the plan and is there protocol to address any fine-tuning that may have to occur?

> Clear about the type and scope of resources you will need *(and have you communicated that need to your ministry superior)*?

> Familiar with the essence of the plan and feel confident that you have a firm grasp on every element associated with it?

> Open to receiving constructive criticism and suggestions concerning the style and method you will use to implement the plan?

> Prepared to share the plan with those who will work with you and can you present it to them in such a fashion that everyone can understand it?

> Ready to remove people from the process who do not have the best interests of the vision of the house at heart?

> Prepared to delegate authority and allow others to make significant decisions that will shape either the success or failure of the plan?

➤ Familiar with the pre-established check and balance protocol that will prevent abuse of power and theft of resources?

➤ Constantly encouraging your team and making certain that they have the resources necessary to get the work done?

➤ Concerned about the welfare of those who serve with you and are you consistently interacting with them, making sure that they too are okay?

➤ Equipped to handle the pressures associated with leading people who may not necessarily like you?

➤ Physically fit enough to carry out the mandate without posing a threat to your own health and safety?

➤ Able to discern what is best for the team and not afraid to act on that discernment?

These are just a few of the questions we should ask ourselves in route to determining whether or not the **'Triplets of Effective Ministry'** are in full effect in our lives. The triplet tools of **Inspiration, Preparation, and Activation,** coupled with our personal life experiences are vital to conducting comprehensive and Spirit filled ministry. We must take full advantage of them as we endeavor to take hold of God's perfect, acceptable, and designed will for our lives.

5

STORMY SERVICE

O n **August 24, 1992**, **Hurricane Andrew** slammed into Southern Florida, ravaging Homestead, Florida City, and other parts of Miami. The storm then continued northwest across the Gulf of Mexico only to strike the Bayou State of Louisiana. In all, Andrew caused 35 deaths and an estimated $45 billion in damage, making it one of the costliest natural disasters in United States history. Andrew's category five/165 mile per hour winds left destruction, death, and dismay in its path.

More than 250,000 people were left homeless, 82,000 businesses were destroyed or damaged, and about 100,000 residents of South Miami-Dade County permanently left the area in Andrew's wake. Andrew also had a severe impact on the environment, as it is estimated to have damaged or destroyed 33 percent of the coral reefs at Biscayne National Park and 90 percent of South Dade's native pinelands, mangroves, and tropical hardwood hammocks. The storm created and left the equivalent of a whopping 30 years worth of debris to be cleared and incinerated.

According to the Federal Emergency Management Agency, the government entity charged with the responsibility of *leading the effort to prepare the nation for all hazards and effectively managing federal response and recovery efforts following any national incident,* Hurricane Andrew did more severe damage than initially thought.

Consider the following Hurricane Andrew related statistics:

- ❖ Approximately 102 miles of power lines & 300 relay towers were destroyed.
- ❖ 25,000 gallons of oil spilled into Biscayne Bay.
- ❖ 7 million fish and other aquatic life were killed due to depleted oxygen levels in the waterways.
- ❖ Eight percent of all Florida agriculture in the southeast region was wiped out.
- ❖ 300 square miles of land and beachfront property were devastated.
- ❖ More than 1.3 million homes were left without electricity immediately following the storm.
- ❖ Approximately 2,200 traffic lights and other traffic control devices were blown down or rendered inoperable for weeks on end.
- ❖ Innumerable small businesses throughout southern Florida were destroyed because of wind and/or water damage, many of which never recovered or reopened.
- ❖ Eighty percent of the homes in Homestead, Florida were deemed uninhabitable and destroyed.
- ❖ 10,000 acres of plant nurseries were ruined or destroyed, tossing South Florida's fragile ecosystem into chaos.

The scene just described is not what someone told me but rather what I experienced and ultimately lived through. My brothers and sisters in the Gulf Coast region experienced a similar episode on **August 29, 2005** as **Hurricane Katrina**, a category three storm, made landfall on the southeast coast of Louisiana, bringing with it a fierce storm surge. Its 125 mile per hour-sustained winds lashed the Louisiana coastline for several harrowing hours.

According to the National Hurricane Center's estimates, it is believed that Hurricane Katrina flooded 80 percent of New Orleans. As of August 02, 2006, the official number of reported deaths was 1,836. The storm is estimated to have been responsible for 84 billion dollars in damage, making it the costliest natural disaster in United States Hsitory. Mississippi and Louisiana are expected to feel an economic affect well over 150 billion dollars for years to come.

It is also noteworthy that hundreds remain missing and unaccounted for in affected and neighboring states including Alabama, Florida, Georgia, Kentucky, Louisiana, Mississippi, and Ohio.

IT IS NOT BY ACCIDENT

The aforementioned instances of utter destruction are not unlike those that we experience in our own lives in the sense that they often leave us feeling numb, confused, and in despair. Still, it is not by chance that the assorted trials, tragedies, and yes, storms find their way into our most intimate and personal circumstances. The truth of the matter is that in the economy of God, our storms are either intentional or permitted. Kingdom citizens are not exempt from the multiplicity of storms that enter our lives and we should do everything to prepare for them. More to the point, whether you are a Christian or not, expect storms and expect them in abundance.

Anthony and **Cheryl Biggs** have been great friends to me for over 17 memorable years. Anthony, a police officer and Cheryl, a realtor moved their entire family from Florida to Georgia after hearing from God.

Anyone who has ever moved from one state to another will tell you that the pressures associated with such an effort are tremendous. Try doing it without having any promise of stable employment, your Florida home still unsold, and without the support of some of the people who purported to be your friends.

This is what the Biggs family endured for well over a year. The strain was obvious as they wrestled with an abundance of issues financial and otherwise. Because they recognized that, their storm was temporary, they chose to *'buckle down and not buckle under.'* They opted to believe God for who He is. God truly proved to be their peace in the midst of a storm.

Because their faith had adequately prepared them for trials seen and unseen, my friends, the Biggs came through the winds and waves, even more in love with God and more prosperous than ever before!

Storms will come!

Those who live in the south know that from June through November, hurricane season is in full effect and its wrath may be felt at anytime. In the northeast corridor, its residents prepare for every December through March for the brutal winter season, which often brings with it snow, ice storms, and frigid temperatures.

Those who dwell in the Midwest constantly stand vigil for violent tornadoes, which unexpectedly swoop in and leave ruin in their wake. Moreover, those who dwell on the West Coast have fared no better as they remain perpetual victims to flooding, tremors, and deadly earthquakes.

Just like our many trials, these devastating and destructive forces are constantly being hurled in our direction forcing us to answer the all-important question.

Will you allow the storms to win out?

WHAT DOES IT ALL MEAN

I am convinced that the storms we have and will endure in our lives, have an intended aim. Scripture bears out that our trials are phase specific. Each phase is sculpted to teach us something about God and ourselves. Life's difficulties do not come to destroy us because if that were God's intent, He could simply speak our demise into existence. After all, He is God!

The troubles we experience are invaluable teaching tools whose sole purpose is to ensure that God be glorified and that we His children grow through the process.

Additionally, these trying life experiences also come to fortify and equip the body of Christ to face and overcome the assorted fiery darts of the enemy. We must continue to render effective service and allegiance to God through it all.

Bishop Neil C. Ellis, the esteemed, anointed, and outspoken pastor of the Mount Tabor Full Gospel Baptist Church of Nassau, Bahamas said in his message 'Confronting & Conquering in the Spirit', *"Our enemies [trials] are necessities. They should not get in your way but instead, push you along the way!"*

Whether the enemy's fiery darts involve severe illness, marital discord, financial hardships, unexpected death or any other concern, they are all geared to teach us about our Savior. I mentioned earlier how the tragedies we endure are phase specific.

Those phases are: ***Storms Bring Crisis, Storms Bring Change, Storms Build Character, and Storms Bolster Courage.*** Let us explore every phase and what they offer in the area of growth and maturity.

IN A CRISIS, CHRIST IS STILL CHRIST

As I am sure many of you do, I remember exactly where I was when terrorists attacked the twin towers on ***September 11, 2001.*** I was in my car headed to the office when the first reports came in, and just like others, at first I was not quite sure what to make of the news.

Upon arriving in my office, everyone was gathered around the television in stunned silence as it became apparent that the United States of America had been attacked on several fronts. Four commercial airplanes had been hijacked and their intended use as missiles would eventually destroy numerous lives both directly and indirectly.

Through this episode more than others, I learned a valuable lesson about tragedy. I learned that ***'Storms Bring Crisis!'*** The domino effect of fear and caution that these attacks set in motion were not only immediate but also long term. Consider the following tragic and mind boggling findings of the **9/11 Commission**, **Guardian Unlimited**, and **USA Today**:

> ➤ The nation suffered its largest loss of life as some 2,973 persons perished on that tragic day.

> ➤ 343 New York Firefighters were killed on that day as they attempted to rescue the occupants of the collapsing towers. This is the largest loss of life of any emergency response agency in history.

➢ The Port Authority Police Department suffered 37 fatalities on that day, the largest loss of life by any police agency at one time.

➢ The second largest loss of life by any police agency at one time involved the New York Police Department, which saw 23 of its officers die on that day.

➢ The maximum heat of the fires at the World Trade Center site averaged 2,300 degrees Fahrenheit.

➢ Fires continued to burn under ground at the site for 69 days following the tragedy.

➢ It took workers 230 days to dig up debris at Ground Zero and find over 20,000 plus body parts *(as of November 2006, body parts were still being discovered)*.

➢ Over 1,600 death certificates were issued without a body at the request of victim's families.

➢ 24 states lost residents when the towers collapsed on September 11, 2001.

➢ 25 nations lost their citizens to the tragic events of that day.

➢ 100 people were classified missing from the World Trade Center that day.

➢ Over 1,300 children were orphaned as a direct result of the 9/11 attacks.

➢ Estimated property loss and insurance costs were approximately $21 billion dollars and continue to be tallied.

> An estimated 100,000 jobs were lost in lower Manhattan following 9/11.

> According to Federal Aviation Administration (FAA), approximately 4,452 planes were flying throughout the Continental United States at the time of the initial attack and had to be immediately grounded.

The aforementioned numbers are just a peek into the turmoil that transpired that day. When people made their way to their respective airports and offices that morning, never in their wildest dreams did they think that anything even remotely similar to this could happen.

The confluence of events, which occurred on this day, brought incalculable anguish to those whose lives it touched. The crisis ushered into their lives by the unexpected and monumental 9/11 tragedy, would be with them for the remainder of their lives.

Whenever unexpected turmoil hits our lives, the last thing we want to consider is that a life lesson may be embedded in its midst. Human instinct and emotions rightly lead us to a period of mourning and anger. The biblical episode found in Matthew 8:23-27 (NIV) displays how unexpected tragedy can suddenly attack our lives while at the same time testing our faith in God.

It reads: *'Then He got into the boat and His disciples followed Him. Without warning, a furious storm came up on the lake, so that the waves swept over the boat. Nevertheless, Jesus was sleeping. The disciples went and woke Him, saying,"Lord, save us! We're going to drown!" He replied, "You of little faith, why are you so afraid?"*

Then He got up and rebuked the winds and the waves, and it was completely calm. The men were amazed and asked, "What kind of Man is this? Even the winds and the waves obey Him!"

The Sea of Galilee, the backdrop for the aforementioned scripture, lies on the ancient Via Maris which linked Egypt with the northern empires. The Greeks, Hasmoneans, and Romans founded flourishing towns and settlements there to include, Gadara, Hippos, and Tiberias, among others.

The First-Century Historian **Flavius Josephus** was so impressed by the area that he wrote, *"One may call this place the ambition of Nature."* Josephus also reported a thriving fishing industry at this time, with 230 boats regularly working in the lake at one time.

Much of Jesus' ministry ocurred on the shores of Lake of Galilee. In those days, there was a continuous development of settlements and villages around the lake and plenty of trade and ferrying by boat. Due to its low-lying position in the valley, surrounded by hills, the sea was prone to sudden violent storms; hence the aforementioned New Testament story about Jesus calming the storm. The main feature of the lake seemed to be its ever changing character.

When the aforementioned and ferocious storm arose, panic and fear also arose in the disciples on board. Through this, we have the opportunity to witness the humanity of the disciples who traveled daily with Jesus.

Despite our allegiance to Christ, when storms come, they come with the designed intent to test our faith but also to test our focus. If storms can cause us to lose sight of and confidence in our God, then they have won. Remember that the next time you experience *'Storms that Bring Crisis!'*

STORMS BRING CHANGE

As I studied the aforementioned scripture more intently, I noticed that the dynamic of the entire story changed once the storm was upon the ship. The calm and serene demeanor which had minutes earlier, embraced the craft, was now replaced by violent winds and waves. *Storms Bring Change!*

We have all had extensive plans and goals on the drawing board, only to have them changed by the unexpected. Consider for a moment how the disciples, who faithfully and earnestly had trusted and depended on Jesus, found themselves in a panic.

As Christians who have experienced the favor and protection of God over and again in the past, we must not allow ourselves to be fooled into believing that He has abandoned us.

Frankly, we can all go on God's record of accomplishment. His history of comfort, shelter, food, and reasonable health should carry more weight with us more than our immediate circumstance.

Storms facilitate change in our lives primarily because they force us into a place of unfamiliarity. To be in the comfort and convenience of the boat was fine for the disciples because they were familiar with its content and capacity. They knew that it was designed to sail and transport them from one shore to another. It was only when the tempestuous Galilee Sea opted not to cooperate and threatened to toss them from their safe haven did they become alarmed.

Change in our lives brought on by traumatic events will sink us if we are not prepared to trust God for deliverance and ignore what appears to be our demise. Often, God's deliverance may not come in the form we expect it to. Sometimes we will have to weather the God permitted storm *(as did Job)* and look for deliverance on the other side of that storm.

Many times, God's intent is to bring forth changes in our lives using storms because every other civil vehicle He has attempted to use in the past has often been ignored by us. The toxic relationships, inappropriate financial dealings, and other poor decisions that we have made, sometimes require a jarring blow to dislodge us from the parasite of sin in order to save our very lives.

Storms Bring Change! Remain mindful that not all change is bad and ultimately, God is the architect and final arbiter of any change that occurs in our lives.

Romans 8:28 (NLT) puts it in this fashion: *"And the Holy Spirit helps us in our distress. For we don't even know what we should pray for, nor how we should pray. However, the Holy Spirit prays for us with groanings that cannot be expressed in words. In addition, the Father who knows all hearts knows what the Spirit is saying, for the Spirit pleads for us believers in harmony with God's own will. And we know that God causes everything to work together for the good of those who love God and are called according to His purpose for them."*

For the believer, there is no such thing as luck. God does not operate in our lives by mere chance. Whatever occurs in our lives, know that God had some involvement in it so that He could use it as a tailor made teaching tool for His children. The monumental changes in our lives brought on by storms have an anointed and specific goal in mind. Just be patient and let God reveal it in his own time.

CHARACTER REALLY COUNTS

On **March 30, 1981**, one of the most violent and heartless attacks occurred when **John Hinckley Jr.** fired six rounds from a .22 caliber handgun at **President Ronald Reagan** as he departed the Washington Hilton Hotel. President Reagan, who had just delivered a luncheon speech to AFL-CIO representatives, was walking out of the hotel's T Street NW exit when Hinckley sprang from a crowd of bystanders just 15 feet away.

President Reagan, **Secret Service Agent Timothy McCarthy** and District of Columbia **Police Officer, Thomas Delehanty** were all hit by the gunfire. Special Agent McCarthy, who protectively lept in front of the president, ultimately recovered from gunshot wounds to the abdomen. Officer Delehanty also recovered from a gunshot wound to the back and retired on a full disability pension.

The 70 year old president was hit under the armpit and was rushed to George Washington University Hospital where emergency surgery was performed in route to his full recovery.

Despite the violence and suffering this episode brought, one man epitomized and exampled how, *'Storms Build Character.'* President Reagan's Press Secretary, **James Brady** was also there on that fateful day and was shot in the head by Hinckley. As Brady lay on the Washington DC Street being attended to by law enforcement officers on the scene, he had no idea that he would be partially paralyzed for the remainder of his life. Although he symbolically retained the title of Press Secretary for the entire 8-years of President Reagan's two terms in office, he never returned to work following the shooting.

After a long an arduous recovery, he and his wife Sarah became advocates for stricter handgun control. The Brady Campaign to Prevent Gun Violence and the Brady Handgun Violence Prevention Act were the result of their hardwork and resolve.

If the story ended there, it would probably still be a fairly good ending considering the positive change which resulted from the actions of James and Sarah Brady.

But it didn't.

When asked his opinion of Hinckley and the assasination attempt almost 25 years prior in a 2006 Washington Post interview, Brady refused to speak ill of the gunman. He replied *"It wouldn't be classy"*. He went on to add when asked how he deals with his disability, *"When life gives you lemons, you make lemonade. I have several stands around here."*

Always know that true character or moral and ethical integrity is built on one's ability to be responsible, trustworthy, respectful, caring, and a solid citizen.

These essential traits speak to our willingness and ability to exhibit an unwavering and holistic integrity for the entire world to see. Although not everyone attends worship services on Sunday, they can still see character displayed in our lives daily. James and Sarah Brady along with their family could have chosen the road of bitterness and unforgiveness but instead opted to embrace character even as the storm raged around them. They wholly recognized that **Storms Build Character!**

DON'T BE SCARED

One of the most formidable obstacles to facing life's storms is fear. Just as fear gripped the disciples when the wind and waves battered their vessel, so are Christians afraid when trials and tribulations converge. As we face these most difficult circumstances, we should always remember that *'Storms Bolster Courage.'*

As a rule, fear generally arises from an inaccurate assessment of available facts. My pastor would often tell us that fear is **F**alse **E**vidence **A**ppearing **R**eal.

Langston Hughes said it best in a poem titled, **'I'm Still Here'**:

"I been scared and battered.
My hopes the wind done scattered.
Snow has friz (frozen) me,
Sun has baked me,

Looks like between 'em they done
Tried to make me

Stop laughin', stop lovin', stop livin'—
But I don't care!

I'm still here!"

Courage stares a storm directly in its face and proclaims to it, 'no matter what you throw my way, after all is said and done and after you've taken your very best shot, I will still be right here!'

According to First Samuel 17 , David was born approximately 1530 B.C. and was the youngest of the eight sons of Jesse. When delivering food to his brothers on the battlefield, young David heard of a challenge issued by the Phillistine champion, the giant, **Goliath**. He immediatley became incensed and sought permission to face Goliath in battle.

The young man came before King Saul and the king relented, allowing young David to fight the giant, who stood 9 feet 5 inches tall. Up to that point, David had only faced and defeated lions and bears who had threatened the sheepfold but David refused to be denied.

David declined to wear the king's armor or use his sword. He went out to fight Goliath with a staff, sling, and five smooth stones he had taken from a nearby stream. Goliath mocked the young Hebrew for coming against him with *"sticks,"* cursed him by the names of the Philistine gods, then attacked.

David calmly selected a stone from his pouch and used his sling to send it flying into the giant's head. When Goliath fell to the ground, David drew the Philistine's own sword, killed him, cutting off his head. When the Philistine army saw that their champion was dead, they retreated and were routed by the Israelite army.

David's resolve to face the gargantuan Phillistine was made long before he arrived on the battlefield. If we hope to face and defeat the storms in our lives, a significant component in bolstering our courage stems from making a hard and fast decision to do as David did and rely on our faith in God rather than on our visible circumstances. It is during these times with God that we are invigorated and prepared for any impending storms because *Life's Storms Bolster our Courage!*

Those who are familiar with my personal story, know how important it was for me to remain faithful to God's direct call on my life. Despite the storms of divorce, ministerial jealousy, and the misrepresentation of my motives, I remained confident in God's strength and continued to trust Him alone.

I distinctly remember those moments as if they had just occurred and how despite the prayer and support of a faithful few, God still placed me on an island alone. I learned so much more about God during those difficult times and as result, I have become my own spiritual forecaster and am better equipped to deal with future storms and tribulations.

Service to God during our life's storms is not easy and frankly, it probably should not be. We must pledge our allegiance to the one who called us and always remember that God has pledged to be with us through each storm!

6

EFFECTIVE TOOLS FOR
EFFECTIVE SERVICE

When I was younger, I vividly recall my younger brother, Chris transfixed as he sat watching, what was by far one of his favorite television shows. The show, *'The Frugal Gourmet' with Chef Jeff Smith,* aired on Saturdays. He would even watch reruns, which would periodically air at odd hours of the day.

You would think a young man as big and strapping as my lil' brother would be watching some rough and tumble sporting event but there he was, captivated by this cooking show. Occasionally I would break away and also watch it with him until I finally figured out what attracted him so much to this show.

As I watched how Chef Smith prepared meals, there was a consistent theme to his work. As he prepared to whip up specialty dishes in his studio kitchen, every single episode of the show found him carefully lying out or having already assembled his ingredients, kitchen utensils and every tool he would require for the culinary task ahead.

As he prepared to work, it was clear that he had carefully inspected and secured every item, and already committed the recipe to memory, almost as if his life depended on it. Chef Smith moved meticulously from step to step, adding each ingredient as the recipe called for.

Every now and then, he would deviate from the prepared script, refusing to be held hostage by it and thus stifling the creative genius that made him so good at what he did. Upon the completion and sampling of his dish, the smile on his face would convey that the intended mission had been accomplished! Today my brother is an accomplished, disciplined, organized, and efficient supervisory electrician in part because of a cooking show!

Go figure.

The tools of those called to the servant's ministry are many and varied. As I mentioned earlier, when I began life in the servant's ministry, instructional materials, guides and the like were non-existent.

I pretty much had to *'grow and go'* as I went along. Still, while on the journey, some spiritual and practical truths became evident to me.

I began to recognize that there were some *'tools of the trade'*, that would make my work and me more efficient. My weekly tasks were monumental and often they came at me with lightening speed. My responsibilities were often dictated by my pastor's hectic and full schedule. Because of this intense pace, over time, several of the aforementioned principles became evident and I would like to share them with you.

SERVE AS IF UNTO GOD

The entire concept of service is foreign to most of us considering the world in which we live. In fact we have been indoctrinated with the belief system my pastor often describes as the, *"he who is greatest, let him be served"* syndrome. Think about it for a moment. You work hard, so you are entitled to play hard, right?

If we accept this logic at face value, it would probably be fine to take it and run with it! Where this argument is severely flawed from a biblical perspective, is its premise. Throughout Jesus' earthly ministry, He heralded the direct opposite of the aforementioned sentiments. Jesus believed that he who is greatest among us should not be served but rather, should serve.

Once, my wife and I took an Amtrak train from Philadelphia to Atlanta and while in the dining car for dinner, we witnessed service personified.

The wait staff wore blue and white uniforms and we watched as they busily took orders and even cleared tables as guests completed their meals and returned to their passenger cars. Now this episode probably would not have been that significant had it not been for something we saw that appeared to be quite interesting.

There was a middle-aged man dressed in slacks, dress shirt, and tie, busily clearing and wiping down tables. I noticed that he was nicely manicured and had obviously made a recent stop at the barber. His cuff links glistened as he worked equally as hard as the uniformed servers did.

Upon completing our meal, he rushed to our table and began to clear it immediately without a word. We could not contain ourselves and proceeded to ask him who he was.

He responded that he was an executive with the Amtrak

Company traveling on business! When we pressed further to find out why he was clearing tables and not relaxing, he responded... *'This is who we are!'*

His status as an Amtrak executive did not exempt him from service. Instead, his status made it imperative that he engage in service because he believed himself to be a servant. If you are looking for some ecclesiastical bombshell other than *'Jesus did it and so should I'*, you will be sorely disappointed. Because he was a servant without motive or a personal agenda, the aforementioned Amtrak executive could diligently render service without any concern for what his critics thought or even said.

One of the spiritual truths about service is that it is never ever about a man or a woman. The servant's ministry should always be viewed through a *'God prism.'* This perspective forces lay members and church leaders alike, not to become distracted by critics or others who work in ministry around them. When men and women in ministry experience personal failures or monumental victories, it really does not matter in the economy of God because it is not about them!

Ephesians 6:5-8 (MSG) relays this thought in a more meaningful way as it reads: *"Servants, respectfully obey your earthly masters but always with an eye to obeying the real Master, Christ. Don't just do what you have to do to get by, but work heartily, as Christ's servants doing what God wants you to do. And work with a smile on your face, always keeping in mind that no matter who happens to be giving the orders, you are really serving God. Good work will get you good pay from the Master, regardless of whether you are slave or free."*

What struck me as odd about this passage being the dedicated English major that I am, was that the word *'Master'* was capitalized. The reason this caught my attention was that the writer proceeds to discuss *'pay'*, which we automatically associate with financial gain. The word *'pay'* in this context was really an indirect reference to the term *'freely give any good thing.'* *'Master'* was emphasized through capitalization because it was not merely a term of endearment but it was more so a recognition of authority.

Kurios *(pronounced koo'-ree-os)* which interpreted from the Greek means *'Supreme In Authority or Controller.'* This not only tells us everything we need to know about God's authority but also His ability.

When we fully accept that He who is, *'Supreme In Authority or Controller,'* is prepared to freely give any good thing to those who labor as faithful, diligent, and God centered servants, we can now see His willingness to care for the faithful.

PAY ATTENTION OR PAY THE PRICE

Attention to detail has and will always be a servant's most important ministry tool. Your ability to successfully concentrate on multiple tasks, will ultimately determine your effectiveness. An example of this comes from my personal memories and experiences at the New Birth Baptist Church Cathedral of Faith International during its 30 Day Consecration held every June.

Throughout the entire month, awe-inspiring men and women come to New Birth to minister in nightly worship services. This annual effort alone has touched thousands of lives through messages of encouragement and empowerment.

At my pastor's invitation, men, and women like **Pastor Joe Cephus Johnson, Dr. Claudette Copeland, Bishop Paul S. Morton, Pastor Freddie Haynes, Pastor Jacqueline McCullough, and Pastor Jasper Williams** come to share. Guests have also included,

Dr. Jamal Harrison Bryant, Dr. Ralph West, Pastor Tony Evans, Pastor Sheryl Brady, Bishop Darryl S. Brister,

Pastor Craig L. Oliver, Pastor John P. Kee & The New Life Community Choir and of course my Spiritual Grandfather, **Bishop Eddie L. Long,** just to name a few.

During a previous 30 Day Consecration Celebration, a guest pastor was reclining in the study just before we went out to the pulpit. He inquired as to the lineup of other guest preachers scheduled for the upcoming week and yours truly, attempting to be thorough, proceeded to name the preachers who had already attended.

He sharply cut me off and responded, "I didn't ask you that *(This of course is the censored version)*!" I quickly recovered and promptly gave him the information he requested and told him that I would be right outside the door if he needed me.

Later that evening after my ego left the recovery room, I reflected on the incident and realized that as hurt as I was and even as rude as he might have been, I had not initially given him what he had asked for. Today, Bishop Curry and I laugh about that episode, which became an effective teaching tool.

Listening and paying attention to detail are essential in the servant's ministry because your sole responsibility is to represent God and your leader as host/hostess, giving God your undivided attention by effectively serving your leader or guest.

Your concentration cannot be split between competing interests. As a result, all of those who were on my staff of armor-bearers made this ministry their focal point. Their time could not be divided between the armor-bearer ministry and other ministry interests; this allowed them to be more effective.

Some of the biggest errors are made in the servant's ministry when we complicate our respective assignments. If your boss asks you for a cup of coffee, it may not be prudent to go the Starbucks or Dunkin Donuts 10 miles down the road. Why not go to the break room where the coffee maker is and make a pot of coffee.

We must make a concerted effort to keep the ministry of service or any ministry for that matter, practical and basic. Stay within your God given talents and abilities and take advantage of opportunities to learn from others who have accomplished what you are attempting.

I have adopted an array of ministry do's and don'ts over the years and I would like to share some of them with you. The information to follow includes insights on:

Assisting Away From the Ministry, Pulpit Etiquette & Protocol, and Hosting Special Guests.

ASSISTING AWAY FROM THE MINISTRY

Serving as an armor-bearer to the contemporary spiritual leader entails far more than just the rigors of Sunday morning worship, Bible study, and revivals. The modern day servant must be prepared to minister to the leader away from the church and through what many may consider unconventional means.

The leader's home is his or her place of refuge and relaxation, so any effort by the enemy to disrupt this environment must be curtailed. Modern day servants should aim to ensure that the leader's home front is drama-free and nurturing. Essentially, armor-bearers and lay members should be prepared to serve at all times.

There should never ever be an instance when we are caught unprepared to assist when called upon to serve. My personal and extensive ministerial experiences reveal that:

Armor-bearers Should Cover The Leaders:

➤ *Home*

-Landscaping
-Garbage Removal
-Adequate Lighting
-Security Issues

➤ **Vehicle(s)**

-Cleaning
-Maintenance
-Gasoline
-Tolls, Registration, Insurance, Emissions etc.

➤ **Miscellaneous**

-Administrative Needs
-Technology *(home office and computer issues)*
-Wardrobe
-Family

PULPIT ETIQUETTE & PROTOCOL

An armor-bearer is expected to serve with diligence, professionalism and most importantly be imperceptible. Like my grandmother used to say, *"we should be seen and not heard."* The same precept should be applied to the servant's ministry. Always remember, *"less is always better."*

When in service mode, the armor-bearer should be immaculately dressed. Shoes should be shined and suits, slacks, skirts, and shirts should be pressed. Facial and underarm hair should be properly groomed. Hygiene issues such as body odor, dental concerns, and the like should be addressed before interacting with the leader, guests or anyone for that matter.

Cellular phones, pagers and any other electronic devices should be placed on silent or vibrate mode. Excessive conversation, even when the leader or guest initiates the dialogue is unacceptable and inappropriate. An armor-bearer should never take a seat in the presence of a guest. Additionally, he/she should opt not to become overly familiar with the leader or guest and their personal affairs. With respect to pulpit behavior, many misconceptions exist and we will discuss a few of them.

Pulpit Considerations:

❖ Your leader's/guest's ministry tools *(Bible, portfolio, towel, eyewear, water, etc.)* should be neatly laid out before he or she begins to minister.

❖ The pulpit should be spotless and free of any other materials or debris.

❖ Determine whether your leader or guest will require a microphone stand or not.

❖ The microphone should be tested and put in a place where it can easily be accessed by you or your leader/guest.

❖ Adjust the climate control to your leader's/guest's comfort level.

❖ Remove your leader's/guest's belongings upon completion of his or her message.

Intangible Considerations:

❖ Do not rush...take your time.

❖ Never take your eyes off your leader/guest.....practice the usage of your peripheral vision.

❖ Move when your leader/guest moves.

❖ Always look the guest/leader/parishioner directly in the face when addressing them. Anything less is a sign of disrespect and lack of confidence.

❖ Complete your task and immediately return to your seat.

❖ Think before you act or move, because you cannot *'unscramble eggs.'*

❖ If you do not know, ask someone who does.

HOSTING SPECIAL GUESTS

Hosting and ministering to special guests invited by your leader is very important. It serves as an opportunity to connect with others in the Body of Christ who exhibit the same passion and love for God that you do. When these ministry opportunities arise, the armor-bearer must remain at his or her sharpest because they now represent their leader and more importantly our God.

The issues that we will cover have been broken down into components that are more manageable. They are ***Pre-Visit Arrangements, Transportation Tidbits, Hygiene Issues, Airport Extras, Accommodation Awareness, Security Measures, Worship Experience, and Post-Visit Follow-up.***

➢ **Pre-Visit Preparations**

❖ Obtain, review, and memorize the Guest's Travel Itinerary. You should be able to secure a copy from the Senior Pastor's Executive Assistant or Designee.

❖ Make sure you are familiar with the number of persons in the traveling party so that you can be certain to have adequate transportation space for every guest and his or her luggage.

❖ Obtain and study the guest's biography and photograph *(commit the more important information to memory).*

❖ Secure accommodation *(hotel)* information to include confirmation numbers, room type, and dates for the visit.

❖ Confirm who will drive and assist with serving the guest *(I recommend that you work in teams of two and its best if these persons retain the same roles throughout the visit).*

❖ Secure the guest's/traveling companions cell/contact phone numbers *(this information should be a part of the printed itinerary).*

➤ **Transportation Tidbits**

❖ If possible, identify the primary transportation vehicle at least two weeks before the visit.

❖ Make sure that the vehicle is weather specific *(sports utility vehicles may be better equipped to handle inclement weather).*

❖ The primary vehicle should be cleaned and have a full tank of gas prior to making the airport pickup.

❖ An additional vehicle may be required for luggage and other bags.

❖ All vehicles should arrive at the airport at least 1 hour before the guests scheduled time of arrival.

❖ If the guest is traveling alone, the armor-bearer should handle the luggage or secure the assistance of a skycap *(a tip of at least $2.00 per bag is recommended for the assisting skycap).*

❖ The driver should never leave the car under any circumstances and he/she should be prepared to politely direct the guest to the rear side passenger seat by opening the car door for him or her.

❖ If the guest has an armor-bearer, escort the guest to the car and come back to assist with the *luggage (the guest's armor-bearer will remain in the baggage claim area to identify and retrieve the luggage).*

❖ The guest should sit in the rear passenger seat and should never have to open a doorknob or handle *(you are an inefficient host, servant, and armor-bearer if your guest ever touches a doorknob or handle while in your presence).*

❖ Once the luggage is loaded, the car departs *(no exceptions).*

❖ Instrumental music should be played at a low volume unless the guest objects.

❖ The climate in the vehicle should be comfortable and if necessary, do not be hesitate to ask the guest if the air-conditioning or heat should be adjusted.

❖ All vehicle doors should be locked and windows in the up position prior to departure.

➤ **Hygiene Issues**

❖ Both Armor-bearer and driver should dress in casual semi-formal *(slacks/skirts/sports jacket without tie is appropriate)* attire for morning and early afternoon pickups. For late afternoon and evening pick-ups, business attire is recommended *(no jeans, revealing or tight fitting attire should be worn).*

- ❖ Shirts, ties, blouses, skirts, and all attire should be clean and pressed.

- ❖ Nails and hair *(to include facial/nose/underarm hair)* should be manicured and groomed.

- ❖ Shoes should be polished/shined and heels should not be worn down or frayed.

- ❖ Cologne and perfume should be used in moderation and not be overpowering or distracting.

- ❖ Flamboyant clothing or footwear combinations are inappropriate and unnecessary *(You are still representing God).*

➢ **Airport Extras**

- ❖ Upon arrival, confirm the flight arrival time, arrival gate, and correct baggage claim carousel.

- ❖ The primary armor-bearer for the visit should meet the guest(s) at the security gate if possible and escort them to the correct baggage claim carousel.

- ❖ The primary armor-bearer should remain in constant cell phone contact with the driver, alerting them when the guest has been located.

- ❖ Refer to guest's biography and photograph as a means to identify them at the airport.

❖ The armor-bearer should attempt to relieve the guest of any carry on items unless they strongly object and state their preference to carry the item(s) themselves.

➤ **Accommodation Awareness**

❖ At least two hours *(for every extra guest, allot an additional thirty minutes)* before the guest's flight arrives, proceed to the hotel and check the guest and his party into their non-smoking hotel room(s) *(Secure two keys for each room)*.

❖ Inspect room(s) for cleanliness and orderliness.

❖ The sink/bathtub should be dry, mirror(s) spotless, beds should be neatly made, and all baseboards should reveal no cobwebs or dust.

❖ The carpet should be freshly vacuumed; closets and wastebaskets should be empty and clean.

❖ There should be some evidence of the presence of air freshener or deodorizer.

❖ Check the face of the thermostat and windows for mildew. If you notice mildew, this means that humidity is seeping in from the outside will negatively affect the room's temperature. If this is the case, request alternate accommodations, *(I often use opportunities like these to insist on receiving an upgrade because of the inconvenience factor)*.

❖ Report any linen, towel, toiletry, iron, ironing board, or other discrepancies to the housekeeping steward. Wait until they have been corrected before departing *(**no exceptions**)*.

❖ Leave opened informational welcome package on any available and visible table for the guest. *(be certain that a copy of the program/workshop/service itinerary is included in the package).*

❖ Upon your return from the airport with the guest, proceed immediately to the guest room *(inform the bell staff of the room number to facilitate proper delivery of luggage).*

❖ Hold open all elevator and any other doors for your guest.

❖ Upon entering the guest room, wait until the luggage arrives and offer to unpack for your guest *(tip the bellman appropriately, once the luggage has arrived).*

❖ Leave room keys on a visible table near the door so that the guest will see them when exiting the room.

❖ Inform the guest of his or her pickup time for their respective service/program and indicate that you will call their room upon your arrival.

➤ **Security Measures**

❖ A gender specific *(when possible, male security personnel should be assigned to male guests and female personnel to female guests)* security plan should be established that will provide your leader/ guest with protection throughout their visit.

❖ The location of the guest's accommodations and any information related to their itinerary should not be revealed to anyone *(itinerary copies should be numbered/color coded and distributed only to those involved in the transportation and guest care plan)*.

❖ Upon arrival to the church or program venue, security personnel should meet the guest's vehicle and once inside wait immediately outside of the guest lounge and never be in their immediate presence preceding or following the event.

❖ Security personnel should be aware of any hidden doors, windows or other entryway leading directly the guest lounge or waiting area.

❖ Whenever a guest moves throughout the building or venue, security personnel are to follow at a distance that will not compromise guest safety or infringe on their privacy.

❖ Security personnel should always have a direct line of sight to the guest or leader.

❖ Security personnel should document any extraordinary occurrences and report them to the proper authorities.

❖ Security personnel should never handle or carry any of the guest's belongings *(the assigned armor-bearer will attend to that)* as their hands should be free at all times.

❖ Any packages given to the guest should be given to security personnel for screening and clearance.

❖ Security personnel should never infringe upon the guest's ability to interact with audience/congregation unless the guest expresses discomfort with any person or persons.

❖ Designated security personnel should be prepared to meet the guest's car upon arrival and see it off for departure.

❖ Security personnel should never engage the guest or anyone else in conversation *(seen and not heard should be the motto on every occasion)*.

❖ No autographs or photographs should be sought with the guest unless offered by the guest.

❖ Armor-bearers should inform security personnel of any special circumstances or itinerary changes specific to the guest.

❖ If the guest travels with his/her own security, then the onsite security personnel will serve in a supplementary role.

❖ Armed security personnel should keep weapons concealed at all times unless in uniform.

> ## The Worship Experience

- ❖ Arrive to pick up your guest at least 45 minutes before the scheduled time and phone their room *(offer to come up and assist with any luggage)* when you arrive.

- ❖ In instances when a local guest will attend, make sure that ample parking is available near the entry door to be used.

- ❖ Upon arrival at the designated ministry venue, the primary armor-bearer should quickly guide the guest to the lounge or designated waiting area identified for their usage *(remember, the guest has no idea where to go, you must guide them)*.

- ❖ Other armor-bearers should be available to assist with any luggage. If none are available, the driver should park the car by backing *(he/she may also pull in forward if it will place the guest's car door near the entrance to the building)* it in a pre-arranged parking space and then bring in any remaining luggage.

- ❖ Once inside, the assisting armor-bearer should leave the guest lounge and wait outside the door in an effort to not crowd the guest.

- ❖ The primary armor-bearer should unpack the guest's garments *(if any)* and neatly hang them up *(offer to have them pressed if necessary)*.

- ❖ If other persons are traveling with the guest, politely have the assisting armor-bearer guide them to their reserved seats.

❖ Offer a beverage to the guest *(do this once…guests do not like pushy servants)*.

❖ Armor-bearers should stand *(never sit while on post)* silently in the room and only speak when spoken too. Any responses to the guest should be precise and polite.

❖ At the designated time, gather the guest's preaching/ teaching tools *(Bible, portfolio, notes, and eyewear)* and escort the guest to the pulpit area *(remember, the guest should be guided by the primary armor-bearer as the assisting armor-bearer opens doors)*.

❖ No notes should be passed to the guest/leader and neither should there be unnecessary communication with him/her once you enter the pulpit area.

❖ Place the guest's preaching tools on the pulpit *(portfolio should be placed in the center and bible to the right)* while the preparatory song is being rendered or if there is no song, right before the guest stands to minister.

❖ Place any beverage on the side of the pulpit opposite their dominate hand *(for example, if the guest is left handed, place the beverage to his or her right. Often, public speakers will hold a microphone in their dominate hand while the other hand remains free)*.

❖ Intercede through prayer for the guest as they minister.

❖ The assisting armor-bearer should guide the guest to the lounge/office after he/she finishes ministering and the primary armor-bearer should offer to cover them in prayer *(this is appropriate only if the guest has no armor-bearer)*.

❖ If the guest needs to change clothes *(and requires no assistance)* or rest, please excuse yourself and wait outside.

❖ If your guest will be greeting well-wishers, escort them to the designated area where this will occur *(do not be afraid to keep your eye on the clock and advise your guest of an appropriate time to leave for the hotel)*.

❖ As soon as possible, have the assisting armor-bearer place the guest's luggage in the car once he/she is done with them *(never leave your guest)*.

❖ When the guest is ready, escort him/her to the car *(car should be on and driver in place)*, transport them to the hotel and confirm the airport pickup time for the next day.

➢ **Post-Visit Follow-up**

❖ Phone your guest or their representative later on the day of their departure and make sure that they arrived safely to there respective destination *(**This will be your last interaction with the guest!**)*.

❖ Make a note of any issues that arose during the visit and notify the senior adjutant or lead armor-bearer of those concerns.

❖ Analyze your ministry performance and be open to constructive criticism.

7

SEASONS

I have always been a presidential history buff. The White House and its many occupants have intrigued me over the years. What is most impressive to me about the presidency is how the institution is designed to pass from one duly elected leader to the next.

An essential component to the transition is the clear and concise understanding that one president's time for leading a nation, shaping world history, and affecting domestic/international long-term policy, has now ended. The existence of this fact is not enough if it is not accompanied by its twin, called acceptance.

I can recall one of the most touching moments that I have ever witnessed. On the morning of January 20, 2001, **President William Jefferson Clinton** departed the White House for the final time as our country's leader. Traditionally, before leaving, presidents leave notes of encouragement and advice to their successor, a tradition, President Clinton upheld.

Soon after the presidency was transferred to the incoming **President George Walker Bush**, Mr. Clinton, along with his wife, **Hillary** and their daughter, **Chelsea**, sped off to Andrews Air Force Base. As president, he would habitually, board Air Force One, the official presidential air transport. Today, as *'Citizen Clinton'*, he boarded a benign U.S. Government aircraft whose mission to transport him to New York's John F. Kennedy International Airport, was titled by the Air Force as *'Special Air Mission 28000'*.

With the niceties and the elaborate trappings of the Oval Office in his rear view mirror, President Clinton commented *"Now we have to go on to the next part of our lives."* He continued, *"Maybe for the first time in eight years I'll be in the driver's seat in a lot of ways I wasn't before."* With those words, the youngest president since **President Theodore Roosevelt** left office. As he climbed the plane's stairs to the top, he turned and waved to supporters, disappearing not only into its entryway but also into the annals of history.

This scene, which has been repeated time and again throughout presidential history, is merely an example of what each of us has had to endure many times over in our respective lives.........***Transition***.

CHANGE IS NECESSARY

The Twenty-second Amendment of the United States Constitution sets a term limit for the President of the United States. It reads, *"No person shall be elected to the office of the President more than twice, and no person who has held the office of President, or acted as President, for more than two years of a term to which some other person was elected President shall be elected to the office of the President more than once."*

I often wondered why this prohibition was only placed on the election of presidents.

Prior to the adoption of the amendment, the constitution set no limit on the number of presidential terms. The United States Congress proposed the amendment on March 21, 1947 and it was ratified by the appropriate number of states on February 27, 1951.

Many, including former **President Dwight Eisenhower** expressed in a press conference, his feelings concerning term limits: *"The United States ought to be able to choose for its President anybody it wants, regardless of the number of terms he has served."*

It has been expressed by those in favor of continued term limitations, that without them, our nation's leaders would become too comfortable and complacent in their roles and ultimately lose their objectivity.

I remember the wonderful times I had as a young man at the **Mount Carmel Missionary Baptist Church** of Miami, Florida. In the 1980's, Mount Carmel was practically the only church in South Florida which held Sunday evening service. Those who attended were not disappointed and were always treated to soul stirring gospel music and a thought provoking message from my pastor.

Usually after service, people would hang around and congregate in the sanctuary and often, conversation would spill over into the parking lot. It was almost assured that we would eventually end up at Jumbo's, Lums or some other local eatery.

One thing I found quite fascinating was the unique *'signal'* we received which let us know that we did not have to go home, but we most certainly had to leave the sanctuary.

Like clockwork, **Deacon McGriff**, a 70 plus something year old man, who also doubled as an official custodian and church caretaker, would begin flashing the lights off and on in the sanctuary until it emptied. If you were slow about moving, he would nudge you along and often had choice words for those who refused to quicken their pace. For the better part of 7 plus years, Deacon McGriff could be found every Sunday evening, faithfully flicking those lights on and off.

Every now and then, we need something or someone to nudge us in order to compel us to move forward toward our destiny. There will come a time when we will have to leave where we are for no other reason than because *'God says so!'*

Change is good primarily because it affords God the opportunity to purge an entity or person of its outdated ways, jaded personalities, and complacency. Often, we can be in place or hold a position for so long, that we become cynical about our mission, and thus our ability to carry forth that which God has entrusted to us is negatively impacted.

The question should never be whether significant changes will occur in our lives, but rather when will those changes arrive. Transition hovers on the horizon of each of our lives and that change not only affects our ministry lives but also extends itself into our personal and familial existences as well.

How we greet and adapt to these changes may determine whether or not God's next assignment in our lives will be successful. Often transition causes causes us to wrestle with and reassess our past productivity. Productivity in the form of statistics can sometimes be misleading because it fails to take into consideration the human element, which is a huge part of ministry.

The people you encounter and minister to throughout the entirety of this season will be innumerable. There is a saying that has floated around in church circles since I was a child. It says;

'Each One Should Reach One.'

There is an invisible element to ministry that you and I will never understand. It involves the incalculable relationships that you and I have developed over the span of our lives.

The people that you have been able to reach, empower, and encourage, also have a sphere of influence and friendship circles that you will never experience. So now, what begins to happen is the equivalent of what I call the ***'Spiritual Domino Effect.'***

When we line up appropriately in God's will for our lives, then those persons that we have direct interaction with become beneficiaries of our obedience. Not only do the blessings pass from person to person but also our families and communities are strengthened in the process because singular obedience will always bring plural reward in the end.

When perfectly aligned dominoes fall in designed succession, each is *'touched'* indirectly by the initial domino in that row. When we fall in line and adhere to the ***'Master's –Master Plan'***, we become the catalyst to others also being introduced to and experiencing God's ongoing favor, even during periods of unfamiliarity and transition.

In July of 2005, I experienced one of the most emotional and pivotal transitions in my life. After having served my pastor as his personal assistant and Senior Adjutant for over 20 years, I was now poised to leave him, my family, Miami, Florida and the ministry I had embraced for so long. My new life of marriage and relocation to the city of Philadelphia was just a few short weeks away.

Those in my inner circle never imagined me leaving my pastor because we were attached at the *'ministerial hip.'* For as long as I can recall, wherever he traveled, I traveled. Whenever he preached or taught, I was right there. Virtually every Monday night like clock work during my initial 14 years with him, we would gather at his home for spaghetti dinners and Monday Night Football, we were inseparable.

Over the last 6 1/2 years, God blessed me with a wonderful group of men and women who comprise the armor-bearers ministry *(my pastor would ultimately designate me **Senior Adjutant Emeritus** and also surprise me by naming the amor-bearers ministry in my honor)* who willingly learned the ropes as it were and to this day, many continue to serve diligently in the servants' ministry.

Elder Robert Tyler, Elder Byron Burnett, Elder Torrence Wimberly, Elder Nathaniel Holmes Jr., Elder Pam Smith,

Elder Susan Ellis, Elder Jeffrey Brown, Elder Constance Miller, Elder Denise Brown and Elder Cynthia Bryant served with faithfulness, loyalty and excellence.

As my time at New Birth began to wind down, I found myself reflecting on the years spent there, and I was struck by some of the things that came to mind. As I approached this season of un-chartered change, I realized that I had learned so much in the process.

As I stated earlier, the changing of seasons often causes us to reflect on our accomplishments and productivity. During this process, you may also be curious about whether you have grown spiritually since you began your walk with and work in Christ.

I noticed two types of experiences being thrown my way and I discovered that this was God's way of letting me know that this phase of my ministry life in Miami was nearing completion. Interestingly, as I began to deal with the aforementioned experiences, I also noticed the intensity with which they came. As I approached the end of this season, I found myself **'Being Terribly Tested'** and also **'Being Thoroughly Thankful.'**

IT'S ONLY A TEST

As God began to transition me from my life of service, some very strange things began to happen. I began to have second thoughts about relocating to Philadelphia and the closer my time of departure came, the more doubt closed in on me. Interestingly, the thoughts stemmed from the misguided (*although I did not know it at the time*) belief that my God given mission had not yet been fully accomplished.

Yes, I had attempted to faithfully serve my pastor over the more than two decades I was with him. Yes, we established a protocol for ministerial behavior, service, and excellence. Yes, the armor-bearer ministry was fully functional and seemed to be well adapted to their responsibilities.

It is true that I had successfully *(so I would like to think)* ministered to hundreds of men and women of God over the years.

Yet, it still felt as if something was missing.

I discovered that it was not so much what I had not yet accomplished, as much as it was the utter fear of leaving my comfort zone. You have to know that my pastor and church ministry were all that I had known for all of my ministerial existence. Now to be on the verge of leaving it all for an experience that did not come with a built in comfort zone was indeed frightening.

My first test was Fear!

Impending and life seasonal changes always bring fear. That fear will almost certainly catapult us into the unknown and unfamiliar. You wake up one day surrounded by strange people, places, and predicaments and are also expected to function in that new environment....quickly!

As I indicated earlier, Bishop Curry always says that fear is merely **F**alse **E**vidence **A**ppearing **R**eal. The many challenges that come to obstruct our paths and cause us to change course have more bark than they do bite. This is not to say that sickness, financial concerns, marital problems, and the gamut of other serious life issues are not real and do not affect our daily lives. If we are honest, it is in these times of *'squeezing'* that our decision making can be compromised and we say or do things we ordinarily would not, had we been in a clearer frame of thought.

My fear found me making bad ministry decisions in haste as I attempted to be sure that we were properly staffed. I even became semi-rebellious and on occasion assured my pastor that I was not going anywhere despite the obvious signs that I was. Whenever I did that, he would simply look at me and respond *"Yeah, right George."* He knew the truth.

Always know that the collective force of our trials and those life experiences that attempt to illicit fear from us, are hardly a match for the supernatural and timely saving power of our God. Because God has deposited so much in us, He has made it quite clear that He intends to see it through. The Amplified Bible Translation of Philippians 1:6 puts it like this; *"And I am convinced and sure of this very thing, that He Who began a good work in you will continue until the day of Jesus Christ [right up to the time of His return], developing [that good work] and perfecting and bringing it to full completion in you."*

Because faith and fear are mutually exclusive, it becomes our responsibility to *"feed our faith and starve our doubts"* as **Pastor Creflo Dollar** of World Changers Church International has implored us to do for as long as I can remember. We can accomplish this through consistent and diligent study as well as attendance in worship service and Bible study.

Whenever our faith in God enters fear's terrain, we should not be repelled but instead invigorated. The new aim and mission should now be to seize the new territory for God's glory and our growth!

Unfortunately, **Fear** was not the only culprit that tested me.

GOD IS NOT THE AUTHOR

Next up to bat was **Foolishness**.

I noticed an interesting shift when word began to spread about my imminent departure. There were those who insisted on attempting to make my remaining time in Miami as uncomfortable and unpleasant as humanly possible.

People began to say outrageous and even mean spirited things concerning my loyalty to my pastor. I began to hear whispers throughout the *'gospel grapevine'* that indicated I was ungrateful for all that he had done for me and that my departure was a reflection of that sentiment.

I was outraged primarily because anyone who has been around my pastor and I for any length of time would know how much I love and appreciate him. More to the point, if they had been privy to the facts, they would have also known that God had already given me my release, an instance confirmed and supported by my spiritual father and pastor.

Some comments even began to contradict God's perfect will concerning my life during this transitional period under the guise of pseudo compliments. They would say things like *"Please don't leave, you are my pastor"* or *"If he lets you go, it won't be the same around here."* First, let us be clear by understanding that my pastor has been in ministry long before I came along and my departure could never compromise that.

The ministry gift and anointing that God deposited in him was the catalyst and vehicle used to speak life into me! I knew right away that disingenuous people were attempting to poison my relationship and destroy the connection that God had established before the foundations of the world.

It was then that I finally realized what was transpiring. The foolishness espoused by those who claimed to have the ministry's best interests at heart was an attempt to cause me to lose sight of the bigger *'God picture'* which involved marriage to a wonderful and God fearing woman, the birth of my princess, Mikayla and ultimate completion of my first book.

I must say that the vast majority of my friends and church family were and continue to be supportive concerning the direction God continues to lead me and my family.

I knew that had I stayed in Miami and not adhered to God's designed and specific *'Spiritual Map Quest'* for my life, I would have never recovered from it. It is also noteworthy that as a result of my obedience, God's blessings and favor on my life have multiplied in the form of a new home, financial security, assorted and pending literary projects, an expanded friendship circle, and most importantly a tremendous and loving family.

While the darts of **Foolishness** came fast and furiously, my next test was equally as difficult to bear.

I HAVE FALLEN……. AND I CAN GET UP

While it is true that God has forgiven each of His children for our sins and past **Failures**, the reality is that the process of forgiving ourselves is a tedious one.

Whenever we sin against God, feelings of guilt, self pity, and uncertainty often overtake us. The endless and agonizing hours of reflection and introspection will frequently usher us into a perpetual pity party minus the celebration.

Dr. Waller often reminds the members of Enon Tabernacle Baptist Church *"While everything that occurs in our lives is not good, it is on good's payroll because it works for good."*

Occasionally, I wonder what would have occurred if my first marriage had been successful. During that time in my life, I was on fire for God and to my detriment, attempted to juggle too many responsibilities. The startling truth is that God has thrown our past failures into the sea of forgetfulness and put up a sign that says, *'No Fishing.'*

Allowing ourselves to be trapped by our past failures has the cumulative affect of interfering with and even delaying that which God has in store for us. Think about it for a moment, the longer you and I are transfixed by the failures of yesterday, the longer we deprive ourselves of both present and future blessings.

Noted motivational speaker, **Les Brown** once remarked, *"You must think of failure and defeat as the springboards to new achievements or to the next level of accomplishment."*

The tool for dealing with past failures is simply to be transparent before God. When we attempt to conceal our indiscretions and fail to thoroughly confess them before God, we are operating in deceit and rebellion. Once I admitted those failures to Him and then made a concerted effort to pursue life style changes, it was as if a dark cloud moved away from my life.

Edwin Louis Cole probably said it best when he wrote, *"You don't drown by falling in the water; you drown by staying there."*

THY GOOD AND FAITHFUL SERVANT

The final and most difficult test I faced at first glance might not be considered a bad one. Because I was committed to the vision of the house and loved my church so much, this test was the most dangerous. My **Faithfulness** was tested.

When you have been serving for as long I have, it is difficult to see yourself doing anything else. The center and circumference of who I was throughout most of my young adult ministry life was intertwined with being a servant. Most of my nights were spent at church or involved in church related affairs and days were spent praying that night would quickly arrive.

My faithfulness and firm commitment to both my pastor as well as the vision of the New Birth house could never be questioned as far as I was concerned.

That was my problem.

My unfettered allegiance to the aforementioned vision almost derailed God's next phase for my life. It was not that I could not have stayed at New Birth and continued to serve, because I could have.

The problem was that just as I was in transition, so was Bishop Curry and New Birth. Some months after I relocated, an array of other staff members also moved on to other opportunities as they too were in transition.

Had I chosen to operate in rebellion and not move off this stage, it would have disrupted New Birth's period of transition and caused confusion.

Additionally, the capable and dedicated servants mentioned earlier would have been delayed in being allowed to *'make full proof of their ministry'*, a mandate found in Second Timothy 4:5.

Probably the most difficult reality for most of us to swallow is that God has equipped someone to complete the work we began once our season of service is complete. Understanding and accepting this reality is a unique form of honor to God because it says *"Lord I fully trust you to order my steps both seen and unseen."* This uncoaxed and genuine faith in God's divine will for our lives will go a long way toward preparing us for the road ahead, allowing us to use our **Faithfulness** in yet another mission field.

TELL GOD THANK YOU!

During my last few weeks and months of service, the overriding emotion I experienced would have to be that of **Thanksgiving**. I found myself reflecting on my ministry and life experiences. I pondered how those episodes had affected, molded, and directed my life. Good, bad, or indifferent, I realized that whomever I was; I was because God had allowed it to be so.

When processing the entirety of our lives at a particular milestone, we can easily be deceived by the abundance or lack of material possessions and notable accomplishments. If we allow the accumulation of *'stuff'* or the applause of people to become the measuring stick for how or when to offer God thanks, we will always get it wrong.

While the fruit of our labor and the accrued accomplishments of life should be enjoyed, we must never reach a point when those things become the focal point of life and living. Friends, life is not real life unless it is lived. Thanksgiving essentially becomes the equalizer in our lives.

It keeps us in a perpetual and balanced place of both confidence and humility. The confidence comes from the myriad of accomplishments we've realized over an extended period. From them, we are empowered and emboldened to pursue even greater challenges than ever imagined.

Our confidence cancels out the enemy of inferiority and levels off life's playing field because now, every aspiration and goal is within our reach.

Through our thanksgiving, humility comes into play because we begin to realize that all that has been achieved in our lives occurred with the hand of God guiding us throughout. When we understand and fully accept that we were merely along for the ride and that God did all of the heavy lifting, our appreciation for His faithfulness should increase. Additionally, those who are a part of your *'village'* and circle of friends, as well as those who do not even know your name; will take a front row seat as they watch you exemplify gratitude to God. This is significant because lifestyle evangelism is a vital tool, necessary to lead the lost to Christ.

What I do is so much more valuable than what I say because my actions then provide wholesale proof that I believe what I say without reservation. When people see humility personified, it should automatically remove any excuses or inhibitions that they may be experiencing.

True thanksgiving does not care who is watching and is not concerned with critics or negative assessments. Earnest thanksgiving heralds to God our personal and earnest appreciation for who He is in our respective lives. Whenever we recognize and accept a person's role in our lives, we become confident in their ability and faithfulness to do whatever they pledge to do. Essentially, their stature in our lives will determine how much confidence and responsibility we place in them. Because God is God, we should give Him complete and ultimate thanksgiving because of His supreme stature in our lives.

Nobel Prize winning novelist, **William Faulkner** once wrote, *"Gratitude has a quality similar to electricity: it must be produced, discharged, and used up in order to exist at all."*

LEAVE BETTER, BRIGHTER, AND BLESSED

When I left New Birth in July of 2005, I was honestly able to affirm that I was now better off because of my experiences there. During my New Birth season, I attempted to assist in facilitating spiritual growth and development. I forged many life long friendships and relationships and also met people and went places I would have never imagined in years past.

My confidence was at an all-time high and those who were under my charge often reminded me of their respect for both my leadership and record of service. The New Birth Church was and remains a pillar in the North Miami community and people continue to flock there because of the tremendous work God is doing through my pastor, Bishop Victor T. Curry and the faithful congregants who worship there.

My pastor's appreciation and love for me has always been evident but it became all the more obvious during an appreciation service. He and the wonderful people of New Birth showered me with gifts as a means of expressing appreciation for my years of commitment to both he and the ministry God had entrusted to him.

All of this is important as I can now look in the rearview mirror and acknowledge that I am better off, much wiser and of course, tremendously blessed.

At the end of the day, we must strive to leave a season in a more improved condition than when we entered it. When this occurs, it will be proof that we have faced, defeated, and learned from the challenges found in its midst. We can never ever allow a season in our lives to become all consuming because it is only a segment of the whole.

A good friend of mine and powerful young preacher in his own right, **Minister Tariq Craig** of Philadelphia, Pennsylvania once prayed these words: *"Seasons should not only lead us to new levels but also to new dimensions. New levels can be reached with our power but new dimensions are only within the reach of our God!"*

Remember that no season is ever larger than the whole. The many seasonal transitions that await each of us are not our enemies, but our friends. When we greet them with open arms and fervent prayer, they can only work in our favor.

EPILOGUE

PLEASE EMPTY THE TRASH
ON YOUR WAY OUT

As a young man attending Miami Edison Senior High School, I remember my mother's voice giving me my final instructions as I hurried out of the door in route to beginning another day.

She would say *"Don't forget to clean your breakfast plate"* or *"Did you make up your bed?"* Often she would even give directives like *"Be home by 3 o'clock"* or *"When you get home, take the chicken out of the freezer."* While those maternal directives were most often followed to the letter, there was one that I frequently ignored because it had no real significance to me at the time.

My mother would tell me every single morning save Sunday, **"Please empty the trash before you leave."** To me it was a strange request considering the fact that the garbage truck only made pickups on Mondays and Wednesdays. My juvenile thought process prompted me to assume that Tuesdays, Thursdays, Fridays, and Saturdays were 'trash free' zones and that I was exempt from this exercise on those days.

Nonetheless, my mother continued to remind me of my seemingly eternal responsibility to *"Please empty the trash before you leave."*

Once I asked her why she would always implore me to empty the trash. She paused for a moment and sat reflectively on the edge of her bed. It was as if time had stopped and we were waiting for God Himself to jump-start it once again.

She leaned forward and told me that her mother and my late grandmother, **Eva Mae Oliver** always told her that if you do not take out the garbage every day, *"it will stink up the whole place."*

The epitome of faithful service stipulates that we not allow our past circumstances to *'stink up'* or interfere with our present and future responsibilities in Christ.

Those encumbrances from our pasts must be left on the curb for the garbage man of life to collect. We must never allow our failures to be recycled or occupy space in our lives ever again. Let the past be the past and then allow God to be God! When we readily release the trash of sad memories and experiences, then we can take hold of God's bountiful blessings and perpetual favor.

As we continue to move throughout this maze that we call life, our resolve, and commitment to *'Serve our God, His Leaders, and His People with Excellence'* must not be compromised.

Service is so much more than an action because any action must first emanate from the heart. As we seek to serve in the Kingdom Community, we must re-position our hearts to first hear from God. Service is a lifestyle that offers no vacation or sick days. We do not serve to have our names called by men but instead because God has already called our names in preparation for our respective missions.

It is important to mention that the designation of *'servant'* is not only for ministers or for church leaders. Everyday ordinary people who love and appreciate God are also servants.

Contrary to what some believe, the church is not a club. It is not a social organization but instead, it is a spiritual organism. My pastor's words continue to ring in my ears. *"Since the church was divine in its origin, it should be divine in it's operation."*

God seeks spirit-filled men and women who will boldly assume the mantle of service and not shy away from the accompanying challenges. Obstacles will come fast and furiously, but be resolved to serve with excellence. *We can never allow excellence to become an act but instead it must be a habit!* Unfettered commitment to the call on our lives is truly the highest honor we can pay to God.

The act of sincere service removes the gamut of traditional, ethnic, economic, and class restrictions that have defined our society. You can be a servant, if only you allow God to serve both in and through you.

The late **Reverend Dr. Martin Luther King Jr.** summed it up in this fashion; *"Everybody can be great... because anybody can serve. You don't have to have a college degree to serve. You don't have to make your subject and verb agree to serve. You only need a heart full of grace. A soul generated by love."*

I encourage you to embrace this **'Higher Calling and Serve God, His Leaders, and His People with Excellence.'**

NOTES

CHAPTER ONE
AM I CALLED OR AM I CRAZY?

Rabchuk, James. Jesus Anointed At Bethany
26 June 2005
<http://www.wiu.edu/users/miubf/messages/
johnjn121236.mes.pdf>

Forrest Gump The Motion Picture 142 minutes (US) 23 June 1994
Paramount Pictures
Adapted from 1985 novel by Groom, Winston.

CHAPTER TWO
THE HEART OF A SERVANT

Jackson Jr., Reverend James I. Sermon: 'Going From Good To Great'
26 March 2006
Enon Tabernacle Baptist Church – Philadelphia, PA

Bradshaw, Robert I. The Life and Times of Elisha 1999
< http://www.biblicalstudies.org.uk/article_elisha.html>

Fishburne Jr., Elder George. The Servant's Handbook: Prepared To Serve With The Spirit of Excellence
February 2005
New Birth Baptist Church Cathedral of Faith International –
North Miami, FL

CHAPTER THREE
GREAT PEOPLE – GREATER MINISTRY

NBA Basketball at CBS SportsLine.com. **Los Angeles Lakers History**
<**http://sportsline.com/nba/teams/history/LAL**>

Wikipedia: The Free Encylopedia.
History of The Los Angeles Lakers
<**http://en.wikipedia.org/wiki/**
History_of_the_Los_Angeles_Lakers>

Forbes Magazine
Forbes Franchise Values 08 January 2003/ Updated 29 September 2003
<http://espn.go.com/sportsbusiness/s/forbes.html>

Waller, Reverend Dr. Alyn E. Sermon: 'Keep Your Word'
Enon Tabernacle Baptist Church – Philadelphia, PA 15 January 2006

Oliver Sr., Reverend Craig L.
Sermon: 'I Still Believe God'
Elizabeth Baptist Church – Atlanta, GA 07 January 2007

Gibson, Reverend Dr. Ron Sermon: 'Balancing The Weight'
Life Church of God In Christ – Riverside, CA

Morton, Bishop Paul S.
Sermon: 'The Spirit of Excellence'
Greater St. Stephen Full Gospel Baptist Church – New Orleans, LA

CHAPTER FOUR
TRIPLETS

The 'A' Team Television Broadcast aired 23 January 1983 thru 30 December 1986 (Lost Episode Aired 08 March 1987) Stephen J. Cannell - Producer

Tate, Margaret. Social Studies Professor
Miami-Dade County Public Schools - Edison Senior High School Miami, FL

CHAPTER FIVE
STORMY SERVICE

National Oceanic & Atmospheric Administration – U.S. Department of Commerce.
Hurricane Andrew – Ten Years Later
<http://www.nhc.noaa.gov/HAW2/english/ history.shtml#andrew>

Wikipedia: The Free Encyclopedia.
Hurricane Andrew
http://en.wikipedia.org/wiki/Hurricane_Andrew

"The 9/11 Commission Report"
<http://www.9-11commission.gov/report/911Report.pdf>

Templeton, Tom and Lumley, Tom. Guardian Unlimited.
9/11 In Numbers 18 August 2002
<http://www.guardian.co.uk/september11/oneyearon/ story/0,,778399,00.html>

<u>STORMY SERVICE</u> *continued*

Ellis, Bishop Neil C.
Sermon: 'Confronting & Conquering In The Spirit'
Mount Tabor Full Gospel Baptist Church – Nassau, Bahamas

Wikipedia: The Free Encylopedia
Sea of Galilee
<**http://en.wikipedia.org/wiki/Sea_of_Galilee**>

Flavius, Josephus. Roman Citizen, Noted Jewish Historian,
and Apologist
Born in Jerusalem in A.D. 37 – Died 100 AD/CE

Simon & Schuster. "Ronald Reagan...Assassination Attempt"
http://www.ronaldreagan.com/march30.html

Curry, Bishop Victor T. Sermon: 'The Spirit of FEAR:
False Evidence Appearing Real'
New Birth Baptist Church Cathedral of Faith International –
North Miami, FL

Hughes, James Langston. Selected Poems of Langston
Hughes **'Still Here'**,
Vintage Publishers 12 September 1990

CHAPTER SIX

EFFECTIVE TOOLS FOR EFFECTIVE SERVICE

Smith, Jeff The Frugal Gormet Television Broadcast aired
from 1988 thru 1997 - Broadcast on (PBS) Public Broadcast
System

CHAPTER SEVEN
SEASONS

"Transition to a New Presidential Administration"
<http://www.opm.gov/transition/trans20r-ch1.htm>

Twenty-second Amendment of the United States Constitution
Proposed 21 March 1947 – Ratified 27 February 1951

Dollar, Dr. Creflo. Pastor, World Changers Church International
Atlanta, Georgia

Waller, Reverend Dr. Alyn E. Pastor, Enon Tabernacle Baptist Church
Philadelphia, PA

Clinton, President William Jefferson
Forty Second President of the United States of America
20 January 1993 through January 2001

Eisenhower, President Dwight David
Thirty Forth President of the United States of America
20 January 1953 through January 1961

Cole, Edwin Louis. Founder, Christian Men's Network
Born in Dallas, Texas in 1922 – Died 27 August 2002

Brown, Les. Motivational Speaker
Born in Miami, Florida in 1945

SEASONS continued

Faulkner, William Cuthbert, Nobel Prize Winning Novelist
Born 25 September 1897 – Died 06 July 1962

Craig, Minister Tariq
Enon Tabernacle Baptist Church – Philadelphia, PA 31
December 2006

EPILOGUE

PLEASE EMPTY THE TRASH ON YOUR WAY OUT

Curry, Bishop Victor T., Senior Pastor/Teacher
New Birth Baptist Church Cathedral of Faith International
North Miami, FL

King Jr., Reverend Dr. Martin Luther. Pastor, Civil Rights
Activist, Writer
Born 29 January 1929 – Assassinated & Died 04 April 1968

Fishburne Jr., Elder George.
The Servant's Handbook: Prepared To Serve With The Spirit of
Excellence
February 2005
New Birth Baptist Church Cathedral of Faith International
North Miami, FL

(Footnotes)
[1] I suppose Zechariah was substituted for Zacchaeus in the song because it flowed better. It should be noted that there were over twenty-five different Zechariah s throughout scripture, none of whom are relevant to this point.

The Armor-bearer's Survival Kit

ARMOR-BEARERS

- ❏ Bible
- ❏ Note Pad *(Both 8 1/2 x 11 as well as pocket size)*
- ❏ Black & Blue Ink Pens *(at least 2 of each)*
- ❏ Red Ink Pen *(at least 2)*
- ❏ Highlighter *(at least 2)*
- ❏ Cellular Phone *(with spare batteries and charger)*
- ❏ Your Leaders Emergency Information *(blood type and general health information)*
- ❏ Important Contact Phone Numbers
- ❏ Cough Drops/Throat Lozenges
- ❏ Contact saline solution
- ❏ Eyewear *(extra pair of contact lenses or eyeglasses)*
- ❏ Fiberglass Cloth Lens Cleaner *(at least 2, always keeping one on your person)*
- ❏ Hand Towels *(at least three)*
- ❏ Spare Cuff Links/Collar Bars/Tie Clasps or Pins
- ❏ Spare Shoe Strings
- ❏ Kleenex *(travel size)*
- ❏ Cologne or Perfume *(travel size)*
- ❏ Lotion *(travel size)*
- ❏ Hand Sanitizer *(travel size)*
- ❏ Miniature Eyeglass Repair Kit
- ❏ Miniature Sewing Kit
- ❏ Business cards
- ❏ Mints
- ❏ Post It Notes
- ❏ Rolaids
- ❏ Tylenol/Pain Medication
- ❏ Items which may be specific to your leader or guest

FEMALE ARMOR-BEARERS

- ❏ All of the above *(where applicable)*
- ❏ Comb/Brush/Hair & Safety Pins
- ❏ Lap Scarf
- ❏ Nail Kit
- ❏ Neutral Finger Nail Polish and Remover
- ❏ Stockings *(extra pair)*
- ❏ Wet Wipes
- ❏ Feminine Hygiene Products

The hallmark of a true armor-bearer is one who is always prepared and equipped for service. Your leader or guest must always be confident that you will have everything necessary to serve effectively. Armor-bearers should always have a *'ready bag'*, filled with the tools of their trade. Whenever I traveled with my pastor, I was ready for just about anything and occasionally, just about *'anything'* would occur.

As a rule my bag was not flashy but at the same time, it was not run down. The type of bag you choose is totally up to you but it should be a neutral and unassuming color like black or brown.

Additionally, any writing instruments, keys, and cell phones should be easily assessable. The bag should be small enough to not be a nuisance but large enough to carry documents that your leader or guest may require while in transit

Recommended Literature

***A Higher Calling: Serving God, His Leaders,
and His People With Excellence
ISBN-13: 978-0-9792511-0-8
ISBN-10: 0-9792511-0-9
Fishburne Jr., Elder George

*** Enjoy Your Journey
ISBN: 0875088244
Quest for a Deeper Relationship With Christ
Waller, Reverend Dr. Alyn E.

***God's Armor-bearer
ISBN: 089274-7234
Nance, Terry

***Ministerial Ethics and Etiquette
ISBN: 0880192224
Maxey, I. Parker

*** Ministerial Ethics and Etiquette
ISBN: 0687270340
Harmon, Nolan B.A.

***God's Last Day Armor-bearers
ISBN: 1892352133
Cooper, William

***Proper Attitudes Toward Leadership
ISBN: 0883686503
Gool, Robyn

***Who's Ready for a Spiritual Promotion?
ISBN: 0962143677
Rettner, Rick

*** Maximize The Moment
ISBN: 0399145656
Jakes, Bishop T. D.

*** Etiquette for Lay Ministers
Martin, Reverend Robert

About the Author

A dedicated and faithful servant of Christ, **Elder George Fishburne Jr.** continues to stand tall as one of God's premier servants, leaders, bible expositors, counselors, vocalists, and authors. Through his symposiums and seminars, Elder Fishburne instructs and motivates the faithful to become consistent and committed servants in not only ministry but also their respective daily lifestyles. Elder Fishburne is a long time substance abuse and relationship-counseling professional who has provided invaluable Biblical insight and wise counsel to countless individuals and couples.

As a founding member of the New Birth Baptist Church Cathedral of Faith International in North Miami, Florida, Elder Fishburne faithfully served as Senior Adjutant and Personal Assistant to Bishop Victor T. Curry for over two decades. He has authored insightful literary works including, **A Higher Calling: Serving God, His Leaders, and His People With Excellence and**  **it's companion piece, A Higher Calling Serving God, His Leaders, and His People With Excellence Guide and Workbook.**

Elder Fishburne, his wife Tremelle and their daughter, Mikayla, reside in Atlanta, Georgia.